ANTHONY ADORÉ

FRACTIONS
of the
SOUL

A TALE OF ROCKS AND BLADES

This publication is meant as a source of valuable information for the reader; however, it is not meant as a substitute for direct expert assistance. If such a level of assistance is required, the services of a competent professional should be sought. This is a work of fiction. Unless otherwise indicated, all the names, characters, businesses, places, events, and incidents in this book are either the product of the author's imagination or used in a fictitious manner. Any resemblance to actual persons, living or dead, or actual events is purely coincidental.

Keywords: #apprentice, #bible, #blade, #christ, #christian, #deduction, #dialogue, #emotion, #evolution, #female, #finitude, #god, #intellect, #jesus, #love, #man, #observation, #passion, #perception, #philosophy, #psychology, #reason, #relationship, #relationships, #secrets, #seduction, #solitude, #submission, #surrender, #teacher, #truth, #whetstone, #wisdom, #woman

Ordering Information:
For details, visit http://www.anthonyadore.com.

Print ISBN: 978-1-09834-356-9

eBook ISBN: 978-1-09834-357-6

Printed in the United States of America on SFI-Certified paper.

First Edition

DEDICATION

I dedicate these words to my heirs. May you assemble the fractions of my soul imprinted upon the threads, breadcrumbs, data points, and fruits I leave within these pages so that you can find me after I am gone.

CONTENTS

INTRODUCTION

The human heart is complicated. You could believe all the right things, say all the right things, and do all the right things and still wind up in an unexpected place. Perhaps some minute variable was left unaccounted for or some overlooked nuance escaped proper exploration and understanding. Maybe miscommunication influenced the unfolding of events: I recall occasional times during prior conversations when her squinted eye, furrowed brow, or crossed arm screamed at me through tightened lips. I took note but did not want to slow the conversation's momentum by addressing each discrepancy as it appeared. I knew that she would eventually reinterpret our journey together after arriving at the destination of my design, as the growth of the heart makes sense in only retrospect.

Between man and woman, there are many complications woven into the fabric of communication. First, both speaker and listener must desire and consent to enter a conversation. Any conversation without prior consent will feel forced and inauthentic, and words uttered within this frame are sure to be met with some combination of defense and dismissal. Eventually, one approaches the other. Perhaps one knows the other beforehand, but perhaps not. Maybe either one has some abstract idea about the content of the conversation beforehand, but maybe not.

Whatever the case, desiring and consenting to enter a conversation with the other presupposes that one possesses a certain kind of openness to the other. And within this openness, one allows themselves to become vulnerable to the consequence of the verbal exchange. When a man and a woman consent to openness, the speaker and listener agree to both receive words *from* the other and contribute their own words *to* the other. This shared dynamic oscillates between vulnerability and confidence: openness to the other means being personally vulnerable to having one's words interpreted by the other. Openness also means being confident in the sharing of one's own private insights through words with the other. A certain confident willingness to be open and vulnerable to the other precedes the first spoken word.

Second, in a practical sense, both speaker and listener, both man and woman, must share the same verbal language. Otherwise, each would greet the other's foreign tongue with a nervous smile marred with confusion and polite expectation. Each, outside of their native element, will assess the other's verbal cues and body language to the best of their ability using existing environmental–societal interpretive frameworks. And after a few awkward moments, when the presence of a language barrier has become quite explicit, one or the other will begin to act out their words with charades in a fumbling attempt to arrive at a shared understanding. The degree to which each understands the other will depend upon their mastery of a common language coupled with a common intent.

Third, within the fabric of communication, complications between man and woman are inversely proportional to the degree of rigor and fidelity that one implements to understand and interpret his or her own thoughts and feelings. What this means is that communication errors tend to increase as one's rigor and precision of internal examination concerning personal thoughts and feelings decrease; that errors in communication between man and woman also tend to decrease as one's investigative rigor and precision to uncover nuanced personal meaning increase. For example, an unexamined life[1] illustrates a certain lack of self-awareness and general laziness, euphemistically described as "being content with one's self," whereas a contemplative life expends considerable amounts of energy in pursuit of clarity, truth, and linguistic precision during a struggle to bring order to internal chaos. Man and woman communicate better with each other when each embrace internal rigor and precision concerning their thoughts and feelings. When one or both live an unexamined life, the light between them dims.

Either through willful ignorance or through feeble development, those with inadequate self-awareness either cannot or will not dissect and categorize and subcategorize personal thoughts and emotions—their curiosity is blunted by the acceptance of mediocrity, their existence apathetic toward investigating the nuanced facets of their own mind and heart, their deliberate ignoring of emotional and intellectual distinctions, their smoothing over of meaningful gradations for simplicity's sake, and their describing of the loose clumpings of similar thoughts and feelings with the same word. For simpletons, life's axiom is to *seek pleasure and avoid pain*. Very little distinguishes simple people from the common animals who follow instinctual programming. Existence, for both, consists of sleeping, eating, excreting, and reproducing.

Human beings, on the other hand, possess an awareness that controls instinct.[2] This awareness, this consciousness, makes it possible for man and woman to perceive truth, find patterns using deductive rea-

---

1   P., Cooper, J. M., & Grube, G. M. A. (2002). *Plato: Five dialogues: Euthyphro, Apology, Crito, Meno, Phaedo* (2nd ed.). Hackett Publishing Company, Inc. (Plat. Apology 38a).

2   Herbert, F. (2005). *Dune* (40th Anniversary ed.). Ace.

soning, and imagine abstract potentiality found in concepts such as philosophy, mathematics, and the future. This special awareness also enables them to choose to *endure pain and avoid pleasure*, in contradistinction from those simple people and animals bound to instinct, for a greater purpose. Meaning, for human beings, unfolds within the framework of time and mortality; they incorporate the knowledge of the dead into their lives, building upon the insights of those who came before, in search of a wisdom greater than themselves. Each is conscious of their consciousness and can choose to focus it on their mental and emotional tapestry to perceive the woven intricacies therein. Using concise language to describe the numerous facets of thoughts and emotions allows them to understand and communicate their interior world to one another with clarity, precision, and resonance.

All would be well and good if both man and woman shared the same understanding and interpretation throughout the ebb and flow of communication. Two simpletons or animals relate quite easily and predictably on the instinctual level because they use the simplest sounds to communicate their intent to eat, sleep, excrete, and mate; two humans, on the other hand, appreciate the complexities of the mind and heart and will continually strive for better clarity through actions and words. However, when differences in meaning and interpretation arise between speaker and listener—between a human who commands their instincts and a human who is commanded *by* their instincts—the fourth complication rises to the surface. Whereas the third complication revolved around one's willful or accidental inability to understand themselves with depth, rigor, and precision, the fourth complication appears from the listener's contamination of the speaker's meaning with his or her sedimented interpretation. All people, human and simpleton alike, make this mistake from time to time.

Even if I were to convey information with perfect form supported by both scientific fact and philosophical truth, success of her understanding me is not guaranteed. Success is never guaranteed. For it is my goal for her to understand and interpret my words as I say them in just the way that I mean them. After she evolves to possess greater perceptual clarity, she will be open enough to see the unique teaching soul that chose to involve himself with her. Until then, from her perspective, I am but one man among the many men already in her life. My greatest weakness is that all my deepest insights and all my best intentions must first pass through her filter before they can take root and make a new home within her heart. At the end of the day, my success or failure with her growth depends upon her willingness to restructure her existing way of *seeing*—her way of creating meaning for herself—in order to make way for the new way of thinking, feeling, and perceiving I teach.

There is an inherent problem with communication between all men and women in general and between the two of us in particular. Communication is always so limited, messy, unsophisticated, complicated, and delicate. Hard work and many conversations are needed before the right words describe our corresponding feelings in a way that our words and feelings show themselves from themselves in just the way each of us means for them to show themselves from themselves.[3] The opportunities to fail and misinterpret each other in this endeavor outnumber the chances for us to succeed. Misunderstanding one another is easy regardless of intention; oftentimes, I even misunderstand myself in the heat of the moment and choose incorrect words during a dialogue. I imagine that she does the same. If we both misunderstand ourselves and each other, the complexities between us would compound upon

---

3   Heidegger, M. (2008). *Being and time* (Reprint ed.). Harper Perennial Modern Classics.

themselves and take on a life of their own; communication that began with pure intentions would mutate into confused malfeasance. If either of us cling to our habitual way of interpreting intentions and words, growth and clarity through conversation is doomed to be superficial.

I have the power to love, she has the power to reject.

Such rejection heightens the potential for emotional death, with a certain vulnerability to emotional pain and abandonment. Her ability to dismiss my sincerity confines the movement of my words within her mind and heart and imposes limitations I never meant to let exist. I am as authentic or disingenuous as she desires me to be, even though I cannot be both at the same time in the same respect. What is my alternative? Shall I resort to crafty manipulation or shall I somehow compel her to accept me against her will? This would not be love. Love is free—free to accept or reject. Risk dwells in the landscape between the either-or of acceptance or rejection. The potential of what *could* be translates into what she *allows* to be. Her hope, will, purpose, competency, fidelity, love, care, and wisdom will either synchronize and resonate with my own or will serve to amplify the discord between us. In the beginning, the likelihood of either possibility balances equally; both acceptance and rejection depend upon what I am willing to give and what she is willing to take.

> *In truth I tell you, if your faith is the size of a mustard seed you will say to this mountain, "Move from here to there," and it will move; nothing will be impossible for you.*
>
> —Matthew 17:20

“

The most interesting things about people are found in the things that they do not want you to know.

FRACTIONS OF OBSERVATION

To investigate the primordial relationship between man and woman, teacher and student will primarily use their imagination to apprehend, dissect, and explore the obvious. Empathy, imagination, imaginative variation, and qualitative interpretation, usually not considered tools in a traditional scientific sense, will be their instruments. Because the accuracy of these instruments depends on the teacher's and the student's clarity during their use, their task will be to identify structures in their consciousness that either impede or enable clarity. Validity reflects the congruence between the observer's analysis and his student's agreement as determined by the reader. The reader shall witness the deductive critical analysis illuminated between the two.

I am not sure where things went wrong. No one starts a serious relationship expecting it to end. But some do and I find it weird every time. You see, most couples seem to embody a certain childlike enthusiasm and giddiness at the beginning because, if for no other reason, things between them are new and fresh. Novelty colors sights, sounds, smells, tastes, touches, and responses to being touched. New relationships are different. They are exciting. And they feel good.

Each individual in the new dyad acts and reacts in their own habitual way to the other while simultaneously gorging on the novelty emanating from the other, enabling each to see themselves anew. New flesh reincarnates innate desire, lust, attraction, and anticipation within a heart pining to end winter's loneliness. Their phoenix is now reborn, rising from its own ashes in the presence of someone new. New possible futures shine forth as flames from ash and, for the first time in a long time, icy passions warm and loneliness recedes.

But I know that there is nothing new under the sun.[4] Millions, if not billions, have done such things in the past. Literature records ample proof spanning centuries and cultures concerning men pursuing women and women running away from men until allowing themselves to be caught. I believe that man's desire for companionship and woman's acceptance or rejection of man traces back to the interaction between Adam and Eve and I believe that their progeny also inherited numerous shadowy memories of Eden from their parents, including Adam's yearning and loneliness, Eve's submission to her own desires and narcissism, and Lucifer's defilement. However, humanity inherited more than just their darkness; we also inherited faint memories of a time before the fall, now blurred through the veil of death and sin.

---

4   Wansbrough, H. (1985). *The new Jerusalem bible: The complete text of the ancient canon of the scriptures with up-to-date introductions and notes.* Doubleday. Eccl. 1:9.

Proof of this latent remembrance demonstrates each time a person desires something good—a good that they have never personally known. Some never experience love but yearn to be understood and accepted, others living in fear desire strength and courage, and few want justice more than those who experience injustice. How can a person who has never known love, strength, courage, or justice seek something beyond the opposite that life has taught them? It is like a colorblind person desiring to see the world in color. How can a person who has only known black, white, and shades of grey want to see in color—something they have never known? Perhaps those trapped in fear, loneliness, and injustice witness others who possess what they themselves do not and consequently believe that they can obtain the same. In this case, even though others inspire them to believe in something contrary to their personal experience, they still recognize those contrary things even though they have never experienced them for themselves. If darkness, emptiness, and sin express all there is in life, then why do some still seek out the light in defiance? How could the people tied and bound inside the Platonic cave begin to conceive that sunlight exists when their eyes have known nothing but the dancing shadows on the wall from the fire? How can a person want something that they have never personally experienced? How is it that something good provokes remembrance and desire with no prior experience?[5] There must be something in us that remembers.

All possess a distant remembrance of walking and talking with the divine, of interacting with both angel and animal, and of walking through harmonious nature in peace and comfort. Additionally, like a shadow grasping at something in darkness, we remember the divine faculties granted to Adam and Eve, and by extension, also granted to us,

---

5   P., Cooper, J. M., & Grube, G. M. A. (2002). *Plato: Five dialogues: Euthyphro, Apology, Crito, Meno, Phaedo* (2nd ed.). Hackett Publishing Company, Inc. (Plat. Meno 82b-85d).

which allowed them to perceive matters of the spirit with ease. All men are the sons of Adam; all women are the daughters of Eve. To understand the relational dynamic between Adam and Eve laid at the beginning of the world, we need only to study movements of the human heart throughout history and in modern times. And for this reason, we find ourselves together, teacher and student, to study the movements of other people's hearts in order to understand our own. Rather than performing an abstract historical analysis of romance and love, let us venture forth into the world and study the human heart from afar at first.

Let us go to a place where men and women mingle together in a dance as old as time itself. Let us find one man and one woman in a quiet nightclub and observe them. From them, we will collect our data and make our deductions about human nature. We will bring them into ourselves and use our imagination to deduce their motivation and purpose. Lest we build a case study, the more often we do this across different people, the better we will be able to figure out the essence of the human heart. The ritual about to unfold before our eyes seems new from the perspective of each at that table; however, the human heart never changes. It is time for the story of Adam and Eve to begin again with new characters playing their parts.

If you will, please focus your attention on the young man and woman. Notice the effect of his approach on her. See how she changes her posture: arms once crossed but a few moments ago now uncross, her pupils dilate, and her pulse quickens as her breathing becomes shallow and more erratic. She shifts in her chair almost unnoticeably. With a delicate touch, she grooms her hair with her right hand grazing her neck. She pulls one side of her long hair behind her ear, exposing her neck, allowing her earrings to catch hints of the low light. With no words spoken between them thus far, she communicated permission for him to enter her space. And with an imperceptible self-congratulatory smirk, he accepted. At first glance, a naïve observer would see only two infatuated individuals exploring one another through playful touch and idle conversation. And while not entirely incorrect, the layperson's casual glance reveals just as much as it conceals, and as such, in contrast with the amateur's way of seeing, we observers desire to follow the evidence to its implication. Awareness of our inherent perceptual deficits motivates us to look at mundane events in an uncommon manner to achieve an understanding beyond a mere complacency with the self-evident.

Let us pause time and halt the courtship unfolding before us with our mind and ponder the conditions of possibility that made such an interaction meaningful and possible in the first place.

You and I are just two observers wanting to understand the cosmos that already exists between man and woman and the new universe created after they have interacted with one another. This desire to understand motivates us to become a special kind of scientist. Information collection, for us, happens by observation alone without the informed consent of either the people we observe or those with whom we have personal interaction. The reason for such a covert approach resides in my personal belief that people tend to change their normal behavior in order to present themselves in a more positive light after they realize that they are being observed in an information-gathering kind of way. While revelatory and descriptive about the observed to some degree, it is more efficient for us to begin collecting our observations without their knowledge. Should they discover our purpose along the way, we would at least have an established comparative context within which to evaluate the change in behavior.

We are not violating scientific ethics because our observations come from what people do and say in public settings. It is possible that our observations will capture attempts to skew the other's interpretation, especially at the genesis stage. Over the course of repeated observations, however, shifts in their behavior will become more pronounced, unless we too begin to believe what the other wants us to see. While forming a personal emotional attachment to the observed would allow us to perceive facets about them normally hidden from frontal scrutiny, we must begin at a distance lest we filter our intellectual effort through our emotional limbic brain. The other in their relationship, already caught in the limbic spell, fails to notice the other's nuance out of willful neglect, pure ignorance, or neurochemical delight. The anticipation that their newfound companion creates for them satisfies their evolved biological mandate: to mate and reproduce ... to multiply.

Observers, on the other hand, cannot strap themselves to their ship's mast like Odysseus to hear the siren's song *and* maintain a proper frame of mind. For if we hear emotion's song, millions of years of evolution would compel us to abandon reason and jump into the sea. No, it is better to begin observing from afar in disguise, hiding our intelligence and intention as Odysseus did during his long return to Ithaca.[6] We will conduct ourselves hidden in plain sight, as it were, and will use our senses to gather information.

I propose that we begin our examination of this meeting between this man and this woman along the push and pull of individuality and sociality. It is important to understand that each brings a preexisting world hidden in the obvious with them to their encounter with the other. While the moment appears to be privately shared between two individuals, there

---

6   Homer. (2018). *The odyssey* (1st ed.). W. W. Norton & Company.

are dozens more people in attendance. You see, the man and the woman over there divide themselves across numerous versions of themselves, with each version uniquely identifiable through each relationship they already have or had with someone else.

What amateurs see is one man and one woman. However, know that the senses deceive without further interrogation and that the human heart is legion—many within one. No one's heart is a *tabula rasa*, i.e., a blank slate, because their heart already has words scribbled upon it when they encounter the other for the first time. Each has had their share of prior feelings, memories, and experiences with other people—ghosts of *who they were with others* and ghosts of *who others were with them*—and these ghosts haunt the meeting between the living unfolding here and now. What observers see are multiple fractions of individuals intertwined with other multiple fractions.

As an observer, you must develop new eyes to see the legions of ghosts influencing the living and new ears to hear their echo. More information will come to light after you develop the skills to hear unspoken words and deduce motivations unknown to the observed. Multiple observations over time throughout their multiple relationships with others are key for revealing their themes and patterns as they themselves are either unaware of their habitual presence or unwilling to communicate it forthrightly. Perhaps it might help to think of the individual as a tapestry and each of their relationships as a thread within that tapestry.

Teasing out each relational thread from the individual's tapestry for detailed analysis would allow us to advance hypotheses concerning the tapestry's thematic unity from its composition. Using this approach would enable us to entertain speculations and deductions concerning how each part makes sense from the context of the whole and how the whole makes sense from the context of each part. Although performing formal existential-phenomenological qualitative research[7] exceeds the scope and purpose of our investigation, borrowing and implementing certain fundamentals from the method will prove useful on our journey to investigate, unravel, interpret, and understand the phenomenon unfolding in the space between the man and woman sitting across from one another.

We should agree thus far with the deduction that both the man and the woman bring an already established world of social involvements with them to their meeting with someone new. No one is an island unto themselves but rather already finds themselves to more or less degree immersed and involved with others in some form or fashion. Each entanglement represents but a fraction or one thread of both who they are to others and who others interpret them to be. If we observers knew the intricacies of each and every fraction or each and every thread, we then might be able to sum them in order to achieve a better and more holistic understanding of the individual. However, at the same time, an individual is more than the mere sum of his or her parts or aspects. Common sense dictates that a person's tapestry is made from the sum of its threads, and while in a sense true and factual, implementing a reductionistic approach alone would blind us from seeing the purpose holding all threads together.

It is my personal experience that individuals hide their most interesting threads from either observation or self-awareness in order to preserve secrecy, to maintain deception, or to avoid shame or embarrassment in order to present themselves in a more favorable light. They realize that full transparency has the potential to alter how others perceive them in the least and at most, they know that full disclosure stands to drive

---

7   Giorgi, A. (2019). *Psychology as a human science: A phenomenologically based approach.* University Professors Press.

others away. For these reasons, some individuals withhold, minimalize, obscure, or reinterpret information concerning their current involvements and past relationships, in effect creating holes of missing threads in their tapestry. Should one venture too close to their hidden truth, the individual will defend themselves with anger, guilt, shame, tears, sadness, indifference, or gaslighting to inhibit further pursuit. Therefore, observers must always be skeptical of instances of self-reported data. Recording multiple observations over time serves to gather the breadcrumbs they drop during their interactions and conversations as they conduct business in the world.

Just as astronomers deduce the presence of a black hole not through direct observation, but through seeing how its gravity warps and influences the surrounding space, observers of human nature begin by collecting data from the individual's social environment. We begin to understand a person from how others interact and respond to them. Interstellar objects in close orbit around the blackhole or that pass between the observer and the blackhole reveal a distortion—that something of sufficient mass must be creating the gravity to influence the perception of this object or that object; observing the thousand little nuances in the reciprocity between the individual and his or her social involvements shows how one goes about creating meaning for themselves. Direct observation of an individual's meaning-making structure is impossible; however, its structure can be deduced by seeing its influence on the surrounding people. Whether or not the individual discloses all of their relationships is another matter but careful observation of their surrounding relationships will point to the missing threads in their tapestry. Just as even the most sophisticated instruments of science cannot see the singularity inside the black hole, observers will never see all connections a person has to others. What remains unseen can be inferred but never directly known with perfect transparency.

One's social dimension is perhaps the easiest to observe because by its very nature, it has a life of its own and it shows itself in the in-between of two or more people. All we must do is notice it and collect samples from it. The primal act of copulation provides our first concrete evidence. It is a social activity and resulting babies are a consequence of this sociality. Newborns are thrown into choiceless social situations where they require a host from which to draw nutrients. From a biological and evolutionary perspective, the baby's individuality stems from its parent's sociality. Said in another manner, the parent's sociality creates the baby's individuality. Babies are born and separated from their mothers and placed into an existing social network of caregivers, parents, and friends within a certain culture during a particular moment in time. As the newborn grows, it finds itself immersed in cultural and familial values driven by reward and punishment. Children learn to speak in their parent's tongue and depend upon their parents for survival and education. Individuality is born from sociality.

At the same time, participating in the copulatory social act is an individual choice. Each person consents to bring about the copulatory social event and if either individual removes themselves from the situation beforehand, a third cannot be conceived. From an evolutionary and biological perspective, the unification of two individuals, man and woman, creates the sociality necessary to conceive a third. Although supported and surrounded by others, each child is born alone as a singular being. Its continued existence depends upon it having its own skin, brain, heart, and other functioning organs. What the mother's placenta did for the fetus in the domain of the social, the new baby must do for itself in the domain of the individual. The child accomplishes these things because of, with, and through their individual personhood. The parents cannot live their child's life for them and the new individual spends much of its life making personal choices. When old age comes and death finally takes them, no one in society can offer themselves in their place. Each person dies alone, sometimes surrounded by others and sometimes not. Sociality is the collection and organization of multiple individualities. Sociality is born from individuality.

A history of lived experience forms the interpretive framework through which one finds and creates a home for the other. One cannot see without some kind of lens that focuses the other into self-awareness in the first place, and this lens is one's existing emotional and intellectual landscape. We must take care to avoid being a one-dimensional thinker: the lens is at once both the product of and the creator of emotional and intellectual situatedness. One perceives meaning through their lens, and the meaning that one draws also modifies the lens. Most people are unaware of their lens, as it does not itself stand out in the forefront of consciousness as a thing to be examined. Instead one's perceptual lens focuses and organizes objects both *for* and *to* consciousness, and as a general rule, people do not take the time to examine it for blemishes. Perceptions made through a blemished lens appear clear and common to the one using such a lens to make sense of the world around them. This compounds complexity and difficulty when presenting a new manner of thinking to an audience habituated to their existing processes.

Even if one, through their own effort, were able to focus their consciousness on the structures of making meaning within their own consciousness, there would be implicit and egregious errors and short-comings built into the effort because *one would be using their blemished lens to identify blemishes in their own lens.* Stated in another manner, a consciousness that attempts to perceive itself through itself with itself both overlooks and compounds the flaws woven into itself.

Allow me to further sharpen this point concerning perceptual blemishes in consciousness by summarizing a time traveler's story.[8] As the result of his wife's death, a man creates a machine that allows him to travel through time. He desires to use his machine to travel into the past in order to prevent her death. He soon discovers that no matter how many times he travels backwards, his wife still dies under different circumstances. He soon feels powerless and forlorn in the face of her inevitable death and travels to the future seeking the answer as to why his wife continues to die regardless of his numerous efforts to prevent her demise. In the future, he learns that since his wife's death motivated him to create the machine in the first place, he cannot use the machine to undo the situation that brought about its creation. In effect, his wife's death made the machine and therefore the machine cannot be used to unmake her death. In a similar vein, feelings, thoughts, and behaviors resulting from blemishes in consciousness cannot be used to clarify and expand the consciousness that brought them about. One cannot use the fruits of their personal perspective to find a way outside of their perspective. Solo efforts to improve or change one's self without another person's outside involvement leads one to reinforce their current beliefs and manners of perceiving the world. For this reason, we observers do not rely on introspection alone to validate our deductions. Relationships are needed for growth of the mind, heart, and spirit; one person identifies the blemishes unseen by the other.

---

8   Leibovit, A., Lester, D.V., Logan, J., MacDonald, L., Parkes, W.F., Saralegui, J., & Valdes, D. (Producer), & Wells, S. (Director). (2002). *The time machine* [Motion Picture]. USA: DreamWorks Pictures.

By taking you along with me on this journey, I not only expose my observations for communal scrutiny but also present myself for inspection as the creator of those observations. Opening myself to you in this way gives you the opportunity to see what I cannot, allowing me to correct blemishes in my lens that you identify, and thus enabling me to achieve further perceptual clarity for myself henceforth.

Let us return to the push and pull between individuality and sociality happening between the couple at that table. During their encounter, each in the dyad brings with them their own established framework of caring, understanding, interpreting, feeling, thinking, relating, communicating, perceiving, and believing, picked up from their relations with other people. Neither between them spontaneously creates an understanding of relationships *ex nihilo*, i.e., from out of nothing, while in the presence of the other for the first time. Each one of them already has a general idea of how to relate to others in light of their previous and existing engagements, and they carry *this* knowledge with them to their encounter with the other. Informed by this structure, each assesses the other across the similarities and differences absorbed from prior relationships. New experiences appear in the foreground of consciousness against a background of generalized understanding obtained from relating to other people in the past.

Now choose one. It does not matter if we begin with the man or the woman. A closer inspection of the relational nexus of either will reveal numerous concurrent involvements and attachments both from and to others. Each relationship that he or she already participates in has its own complexities, roles, duties, expectations, and obligations: parent, child, son, daughter, mother, father, brother, sister, aunt, uncle, niece, nephew, grandparent, grandchild, caregiver, patient, teacher, student, friend, boyfriend, girlfriend, confidant, lover, saboteur, enemy, provider, protector, employee, customer, leader, and follower, to name a few. Individuals often find themselves immersed in many of these roles and relationships simultaneously—each with its own rules of bonding and attaching to the other. Their numerous relationships and the countless facets therein at once remain distinct yet overlap with one another across the chaotic harmony in one's heart and mind; individuals find, define, and create meaning for themselves at the intersection of their social involvements.

Each person at that table inhabits more than one role, with each role occupied demanding its own unique interactions at different moments with different people. At the same time, however, individuality weaves the threads from each of these divergent roles into a singular tapestry, the self. Every relational thread therein is a microcosm into itself, distinguished from others, and yet still part of a greater whole. Observers must understand that threads and tapestries contextualize each other: when one is in the foreground of attention, the other is in the background of consciousness; when one is in focus, the other is out of focus. Deductions about one always imply deductions about the other. Exploring one leads to discoveries about the other. We began this investigation of the individual along their social dimension. However, exploring the social throws us toward the individual, which in turn hurls us back toward the social. Observing others means dancing in the whirlwind of their individual and social expectations and involvements.

Observers must also understand that each person sitting at the table orients and situates themselves within each of their numerous involvements with intellect and emotion, i.e., with *attunement*. She might distrust her father yet love her mother. He might express resentment toward a brother yet respect his employer. The emotional and intellectual facets within each relationship are numerous and sometimes contradictory, yet each facet reveals and conceals different dimensions of their author and shows that one person is able to entertain divergent thoughts and feelings simultaneously. Some feelings and thoughts appropriate to one relationship are inappropriate in others, whereas similar thoughts and feelings are found across multiple relationships. He might feel gratitude both toward his father and his wife while feeling anger toward his neighbor. She might hate both her church minister and a past suitor while feeling tender and kind toward her brother. Each person splits themselves across many involvements, and each involvement has thoughts and feelings that make sense within the context of that particular involvement. The individual then calls each of their involvements back home to themselves, contradiction and noncontradiction alike, transcribing the legion of their social entanglements with their singular body, mind, and soul.

Feelings and thoughts from these involvements follow the individual to solitude's door where he or she either invites them in or leaves them standing outside. At times they are ambassadors of clarification and insight, while at other times, they are harbingers of pain and sorrow. Memory calls them from their resting place and imagination clears their path forward. Their primordial ties to consciousness itself pull them in through the space under the door or through the keyhole, discarding any conscious effort to keep them away. They refuse to be dismissed and will make themselves known through interior dialogue, whether or not the individual sleeps. For the most part, people tacitly know the "what" and "why" of their behavior even if their dialogue communicates otherwise.

Patterns begin to emerge across one's interior landscape between their feeling, thinking, and behaving in relation both to themselves and to others. In short, patterns emerge within one's *understanding*. It is important to pay attention when the same feelings or thoughts visit repeatedly within individuality; it is also important to notice repetition in how others appear to individuality and how individuality appears to others. Both are abundant wells of information. Both appear through a certain kind of understanding. She might harbor anger and resentment toward *all* men or men with a certain commonality in age, race, eye color, height, style, weight, or some other accidental feature. Meanwhile, he overly attaches himself to any female who shows him the least bit of attention and immediately changes his interests to match hers. Patterns reveal understanding and interpretation—how one situates themselves in their world of involvements.

Repeated exposure to others along established roles grows and reinforces one's habitual presence and also one's habitual attunement. One finds themselves and understands themselves in the world in a certain manner along predictable social and individual dimensions. Every distinct relationship illuminates facets of how one relates to those in their world and also how those in their world relate to them. Relational repetition with established others forges the template by which one will interpret future others. Within relationships, the tension between one's social and individual worlds enables one to understand themselves; choices made in response to this tension clarify individuality and build the framework for perceiving and interpreting the other.

The appearance of the other also occurs within *time*, that is, within one's architecture of *looking back* and *looking forward* from the *present*. Far from being the summation of one moment with the next in sequential order, time is nonlinear, and past and future intertwine in the present in a meaningful way as a function of how one finds themselves situated in the here and now. As one cannot hold and maintain the totality of their past experience in present consciousness or entertain all possible future eventualities, fractions of the past or future only come into focus as a function of one's present attunement. As one's attunement shifts, different memories surface to corroborate it and, without a conscious effort to enact a new trajectory, the future extends it. Because consciousness is always consciousness of something in the present, the past and future reveal themselves as symptoms or signifiers of current meaning and purpose.

For example, feeling sad in the here and now tends to call forth supporting memories of feeling sad. The future concurrently comes into focus through the lens of sadness and possibly pessimism. Frustration and disappointment in the present awaken past memories of the same and shapes the future for their continuance. Happiness in the present finds happiness in the past and clears the path for happiness in the future. Resentment, pain, and discomfort happening now produces evidence showing its historical thematic pattern over time and colors the future with a similar brush. The established framework of love, lust, attention, and validation in the present beckon one's past and molds future expectations of the same. Even though attunement fluctuates with positive and negative thoughts, emotions, and behaviors in the present, as is natural and common for all people, attention to *habitual* and *thematic* attunement over time reveals a particular consistency unique to that person and provides observers with a window into how one creates and interprets meaning for themselves.

The assumption for us is that observed thoughts, feelings, and behaviors, which, at first, seem to have no root in reason, make sense from a certain point of view. *Behaviors do not just appear from nothingness but instead announce themselves against an existing background of sociality and individuality within time with a particular attunement.* In order to understand others with fidelity, we must first collect and plot a series of their behaviors, named "breadcrumbs" or "data points," in order to reverse-engineer and extrapolate their trajectory to the framework from which they came. Our responsibility as observers is to identify and describe the conditions of possibility that allow phenomena, the behavior of others, to appear. While we accept that the intricacies and nuances—the singularity—within the individual's world of relationships will remain hidden from direct observation, we can still infer them with reasonable approximation based upon how they impact others, including ourselves. We, as observers, must strive to understand and interpret the individual's social entanglements through careful observations and deductions from their given data points. These data points are traces of themselves they leave behind before, during, and after their interaction with others. We can then make reasonable predictions concerning the individual's future trajectory with others based upon their established patterns.

The only variable that cannot be accounted for is *change* or *choices that one makes outside established patterns.* Evidence and numerous observations suggest that most human beings do not change easily or outright. Rather, human beings evolve different improved iterations of themselves over time, keeping certain adaptations to stimulus and circumstance while discarding others. This process is called *adaptive learning.* People tend to integrate lessons relevant to their purpose, increasing the probability and likelihood of actually achieving their purpose. All conceivable events, including personal change, entail a certain degree of mathematical probability of happening as a general principle. The likelihood of any particular event *actually* occurring, like personal change, either increases or decreases depending upon other variables. For example, there is a mathematical probability that a person will spontaneously dematerialize on Earth and rematerialize on Mars. The likelihood of that probability is astronomically small and statistically insignificant, however, still possible. There's also a chance that a person will interact with others today, the likelihood of which depends upon whether or not they get out of bed. As the likelihood of getting out of bed increases, the probability that the person will encounter others also increases. The probability for personal change becomes more or less likely depending on the actions a person takes to bring about their change. Staying within the habitual, mundane, and familiar, never deviating from entrenched parameters, and forming relationships with the same kind of person decreases the likelihood of personal change. On the other hand, doing something different, becoming open to possibilities, and envisioning a future outside established patterns increases the likelihood of personal change. The possibility of doing the same thing and getting a different result is similar to the possibility of spontaneously materializing on Mars.

It has been this observer's experience that most human beings prefer comfort over discomfort, order and predictability over chaos and uncertainty, pleasure over pain, repetition over novelty, and acceptance over change. And while there are exceptions to this rule that arise from time to time, most would rather remain where they are, with all their existing understandings and interpretations of the world left intact, rather than exert the effort needed to change and face the consequences flowing from a new way of being in the world. The possibility of change always exists; the probability or likelihood of change fluctuates.

Real change, on the other hand, entails a radical departure from established patterns of feeling, thinking, and behaving. Identifying whether or not a person has changed, for the observer, means being aware of their established patterns in order to determine the degree of variance from the norm after the "change." This can be done after recording multiple observations and collecting breadcrumbs or data points, the plotting of which will assist in determining whether or not present revelations fit past patterns. When people say of themselves, "I have changed," what they usually mean is that their established patterns have *temporarily* shifted in order to accommodate new information. Data points over time reveal whether or not new habits replace old ones, new thoughts replace old thoughts, new feelings replace old feelings, and new behaviors replace old behaviors. More often than not, after the novelty of a new situation or person wears away, most people return to the familiar. "Better to deal with the devil you know than with the devil you do not know," as the expression goes. For some, the revelation of new possibilities aggravates fear and anxiety due to the awareness of the profound responsibility that one must take for their choices.

One is not simply a passive recipient in life, but the architect of their own present choices, the ambassador of their past, and the emissary of their future. All people embody three versions of themselves: past, present, and future. The realization of choice and responsibility either sets the stage for greatness or offers an excuse to keep the mundane. Rather than choose to expand consciousness in order to adopt a new way of being, fear and trembling drive most to make the choice of not making any choice at all. *However, choosing not to choose is still a choice.*[9] Such decisions made to proceed or regress translate into one more data point. Real change in contrast reflects an extreme response following an extreme stimulus: death or the threat of mortality, loss or potential loss of a loved one, violence or the threat of violence, profound betrayal or heartbreak, or some other significant spontaneous realization where one

---

9   Sartre, J. (1993). *Being and nothingness* (Original ed.). Washington Square Press.

confronts their own finitude either directly or through others as a proxy to themselves. This, too, constitutes a data point.

One finds themselves differently after responding to an extreme stimulus. Sedimented and habitual understanding and interpreting peel away, making possible new ways of seeing, feeling, and thinking. It is like finding a sunlit clearing in the forest after traveling through the dark wood. The world now *reveals* itself differently in proportion to one's new way of *looking* at it; old ways are now perhaps seen as limiting, immature, uncomfortable, inadequate, and incomplete. Old rituals that served a purpose once upon a time are finished; continuing to follow their carved and well-worn path after growing awareness means restricting potential with explicit consent and intent. One becomes *aware* of the boundaries of their existence, and a new choice confronts them: to keep boundaries as they are or to expand them into the unknown. New possibilities never before considered emerge while looking back and looking forward; one is able to see new facets, for bliss or woe, within existing involvements, and for a brief moment, one is able to envision a future for themselves outside of their data point pattern using their imagination.

But experiencing change, expanding consciousness, and taking on new choices and responsibilities are not the norm. Observers should never underestimate the seductive pull of the familiar. After all, the choices one makes or refuses to make are reasonable, or rather understandable, from a certain point of view. And it is our responsibility to illuminate the framework from which understanding comes. One does not stumble across the familiar the same way that one encounters profound life-changing stimulus; the former takes shape through repetition, habit, and ritual over time, reinforced through an existing social network comprising many different individuals and many different relationships, whereas the latter presents itself to consciousness with little to no warning and no prior framework or roadmap with which to determine the proper course of action with confidence. Faith, full-hearted and half-sure,[10] is needed to step into the void of the unknown and deal with the resulting consequences.

Most respond not with faith but with confusion and anxiety when the myriad of new choices accompanying the profoundness initially confronts them. The implication of each choice modulates new ways of being, creating numerous alternative futures, amplifying the weight of responsibility's consequence in choosing one among many. *Choosing one also means not choosing others.* Choices made or not made all carry consequences. Many will falter and crumble under the possibility of taking on this new weight. Their instinctual imperative, rooted in evolutionary biology, will be toward self-preservation: to either fight or flee new threats, that is, to either consciously refuse to change through adamant denial or through willful neglect or apathy when faced with the threat of opportunity and evolution.

Most will choose to surrender autonomy and responsibility in order to find comfort in the familiar. Such action conserves the energy needed to expand consciousness, assigning it instead to invest further in rote relationships and activities. While myopic, choosing the familiar, the path of least resistance, ensures survival with minimal disturbance. Human beings, on the other hand, when confronted with the threat to evolve, have the ability to transcend instinct in order to incorporate and absorb the new information revealed through the confrontation with profoundness.

---

10   Knowles, R. T. (1986). *Human development and human possibility: Erikson in the light of Heidegger.* UPA.

Actualizing the potential of being and becoming someone different means surrendering the familiar in part or in whole. Some individuals might express a certain reluctance to do so in light of their attachment to their participatory role in the familiar's creation. Sacrificing it, for them, also means nullifying the time and effort invested into its evolution and continuation. Other individuals show hesitance for emotional reasons. Because the familiar embodies the framework of how they hitherto created comfort and meaning for themselves, abandoning it even under extreme circumstances might invalidate their sense of consistency and provide the opportunity to call into question why they adopted it in the first place. The thought of scrutinizing past decisions along with their emotional context is appalling to the one unfamiliar with self-examination based in reason.

For these people, abandoning the familiar implies that the original feeling and thinking that shaped their initial attachment to it was somehow flawed or insufficient or that some shortcoming such as being gullible, deceitful, ignorant, desperate, fearful, lazy, or apathetic motivated their connection to it—and therefore all subsequent thoughts and feelings flowing from it inherited this contaminated underpinning. Changing the familiar means changing how one connects to it, how one defines both themselves and others through it, and the comfort one draws from it. In short, as an observer, in order to understand the other, you must begin by understanding what's familiar to them, namely, their existing world of social entanglements.

Something easily broken was never put together correctly at the start; things incorrectly assembled are meant to be broken. There are those who latch on to the familiar out of no particular important attachment to it other than the fear of being without it. It is, to them, a safety blanket—a sanctuary—and a lens through which the world comes into focus. Letting go of the familiarity reinforced by others in favor of something independent and self-chosen involves a certain degree of *personal* freedom and responsibility for selecting an alternative to take its place. It is far easier for people to accept *what is* than to exert the effort to discover *what could be.*

Across time, the familiar blends elements of pain and suffering with aspects of comfort and belonging; it is something known rather than unknown, reliable rather than unreliable, and consistent rather than inconsistent. The individual's only role thus far has been to accept it and, insofar as their personal choice is involved, to maintain and sustain it. The freedom it offers has been handed to them by their existing social network of involvements; others have brought it into existence, and all the individual has had to do until this point is assimilate it into their mode of being. Imperfect and incomplete as it is for the individual, the familiar offers low-effort predictability and a ready-made dwelling for the ignorant, apathetic, sedate, and defiant. After all, something is better than nothing.

But confrontation with mortality is inevitable. Death prowls like a hungry lion looking for someone to devour.[11] One glimpses not only their own future but also the ultimate future of all the living during a casual stroll through the cemetery—each tombstone signaling the clear victor. Stuffed animals, toys, flowers, miniature flags, worn photos, and other trinkets of affection left by the surviving silently testify to death's indiscriminate and gluttonous appetite. Billions have come and gone long before those living in the here and now drew their first breath; all the dead's words, secrets, passions, adventures, memories, relationships,

---

11   1 Pt. 5:8

aspirations, moralities, regrets, struggles, insights, achievements, plans, and dreams are now dust underfoot—dust that the living vigorously scrub from their flesh with annoyance in an effort to remain clean, sanitary, and presentable to others. The day will come when a new generation finds all of *our* efforts just as dirty and inconvenient. As we wash away the treasures of the dead found in the dust, we too will be washed away by those living in the future.

The silent once had a life filled with potential; everyone among them entangled in a nexus of relationships. All knew hunger, winter's biting cold, and admired the moon's glow. Many felt desire, buried family and friends, and dreamed of tomorrow. They served their own self-interests or performed acts of generosity, worshipped a deity above or a deity in the mirror, and confided secrets in friends or kept their mysteries hidden. Many have had conversations late into the night, were interrupted by the rising sun, and decorated their interior landscape with promises of lust, love, and laughter. The pious among them dedicated their mind and body to a greater purpose, while the young and hedonistic among the dead crashed against the limitations of the flesh during their love making. As it is with the living, everyone among the dead was both a world unto themselves in their individuality and a citizen in the world of others in their sociality. But now, a chorus of eternal silence fills the dead's home—their openness now closed, their light now spent, and their tears now dried.

As observers, we must take a moment and step back to consider the implications described thus far. On the one hand, there are those who live according to the principles offered by the familiar. Many of these people refuse to change even under the provocation of an extreme stimulus. Although they possess the potential to transcend the limitations defined by the familiar, fear and anxiety convince them to retreat into the consistency and comfort of its repetition. Their choices are inauthentic insofar as something else, other than their own consciousness, determines their personal agency. On the other hand, there are those who listen when an extreme stimulus speaks, learn when it teaches, and evolve when it presents the opportunity to do so. Separating themselves from the familiar reflects an authentic choice to live life according to their own principles and values. These human beings accept the responsibility of their choices and understand that their *being* is always in a state of *becoming*. Their choices create meaning for themselves while the instinctual and inauthentic passively adopts personal meaning from others.

Everything a person does or does not do, whether authentic or inauthentic, is information to us. Each relationship they have is one more thread woven into the tapestry of their life, and every nuance within each relationship is a breadcrumb or data point to us. Whether we understand the sum of all threads or the unifying cause of the tapestry, omissions discovered from missing threads will still make sense and it will be possible to extrapolate their placement in the whole from adjacent relationships. All threads beckon to their tapestry as the harmony of each tapestry guides the placement of each thread. Each provides foreground–background context for interpreting and understanding the other: thread–tapestry, individual–social, authentic–inauthentic, and life–death. A person brings the entirety of their being, including all their threads, with them to their encounter with the other, and while the untrained eye sees only two people, the trained eye sees so many more. Specters of past and present relationships haunt the living in the shadows of their mind and heart, silently influencing choices, exchanging repetition for comfort and validation.

Each person is both at once an individual and legion, with fractions of their heart given to people in the past and in the present. Most people encounter the other within the familiar, which means the novelty emanating from the other is nothing more than a modification from novelty experienced before. Her feelings toward him in the here and now are actually nothing more than rearranged fractions of herself borrowed from her father, grandfather, brother, past lovers, and other ghosts in her life. She did not begin existence as a companion or a lover, but rather as an infant immersed in a social network. She internalized the lessons that others taught her about love, about how to be social, and other people provided her with numerous interactions necessary for her to develop a sense of right and wrong long before she met her new partner in this nightclub. She carried forward how she negotiated these lessons starting from infancy, i.e., basic trust versus basic mistrust[12] and revisited them during each stage of her later development. Present in the here and now is the fruit of that labor. In a similar vein, any feelings experienced after being in his presence did not spontaneously emerge from nothingness, but rather from the assembled fractions from those she involved herself with before.

His feelings toward her appear in the foreground against the background of his relationship with his mother, sister, aunt, a past lover, and other ghosts from his social network. Each believes that something new will happen in light of the one sitting in the seat across from themselves at that table in the nightclub, that the other holds the promise of a new tomorrow. But there is nothing new under the sun; the ghostly warmth from the phoenix's flame comes from their hope masturbating their desire.

---

12   Erikson, E. H. (1993). *Childhood and society* (Reissue ed.). W. W. Norton & Company.

Some might say that this warmth—any warmth—is better than no warmth at all ... and they might be right. But to remain content and sedate with it, to believe that the first warmth is also the last warmth, that nothing better could ever exist, and therefore cling to what is known rather than search for something more ... that expresses fear, not faith. And the next generation will inherit this blemish from their parent's lens and begin life believing that this understanding is "normal." Their accepted understanding of the world will pass through this blemished lens and will serve as their background that focuses objects in the foreground. The sins of the parents are to be laid upon their children who repeat them out of ignorance.

Understand that death is the ocean that borders this island of the living. Everything that we have observed together and everything that I have discussed with you thus far has occurred within the context of both of us being alive, sharing the same language, and having the same goal of understanding man, woman, and their relationship. If either one of us were to die, the wisdom passing between us would no longer be important or useful as the dead do not share the same concerns as the living. For this reason, it is important to accumulate as much knowledge and wisdom in this life as possible before the breath of life[13] leaves us and returns home. Any knowledge and wisdom discovered in life through careful observation comes at a price to observers: death must threaten to take it all away and condemn us to be forgotten.

The dead's threads and tapestries are now dust in the wind, their fractions broken, and their familiarities are forever adrift in darkness. Ozymandias[14] rose and fell, his power meaningless in the ocean of time.

---

13   Gn. 2:7

14   Shelley, P. B. (2017). *Selected poems and prose*. (J. Donovan & C. Duffy, Eds.; Annotated ed.). Penguin Classics.

However, we can still learn a few things about life from their dust because everything is information to us. Even though the dead cannot speak for themselves, our voice can unite with theirs and they can speak through our interpretations and observations provided that we have taken the time and effort to develop our own clarity and expanded our way of thinking, feeling, perceiving, interpreting, understanding, seeing, hearing, touching, smelling, and tasting. We can repeat and describe what they said and did in the same spirit of truth that motivated them to act in the first place. The spirit of truth transcends both life and death.

We perceive all things in existence with our limits, through our limits, and because of our limits. Limitations are an essential component of our existence. For example, we know that visible light constitutes a small part of the electromagnetic spectrum that ranges from radio waves to gamma rays. Even though the naked eye cannot perceive everything available to be perceived, our average everyday visual apprehension depends upon the eyes' limited and specialized perceptual ability. We also know that some animals are able to hear sounds that humans cannot. Elephants, moles, cats, dogs, dolphins, and bats are able to sense things within, above, or below a human's perceptible audible range. The limits of our hearing constitute our auditory reality. Smelling, tasting, and touching are no different in this regard. We know that a dog's sense of smell exceeds our own, that the number of taste buds varies across catfish, birds, pigs, and cows, and that taste is a function of not only the number of taste receptors but also the kinds of taste buds available. We also know that seals and alligators have a significant quantity of touch receptors that allow them to detect movement through water and that the sense of touch depends upon the number and density of mechanoreceptors, thermoreceptors, pain receptors, and proprioceptors throughout their skin.

Animal abilities to perceive stimuli outside the range of human apprehension and the data from various scientific instruments provide ample proof that our five senses perceive a limited amount of information, and that realms of information exist just beyond our apprehension. However, from this limited amount of information, human beings construct their reality, make observations and deductions, evaluate choices and decisions, and respond to others in the environment. One noteworthy deduction from the structure of our limitations is the exponential degradation of understanding involved when we interact with each other. Communication between people occurs with limits, through limits, and because of limits. Speakers process limited information through a blemished lens with limited understanding using limited words, and then communicate limited ideas to a limited listener, who in turn, processes the already limited information with their idiosyncratic limitations. I am befuddled that people reach any degree of understanding or agreement about anything at all. It stands to reason that even the most profound, insightful, and life-changing ideas about the things our body perceives is based on limited data.

When we as humans perceive anything with our body, through our body, and because of our body, we are not perceiving the thing itself, the noumenon, because our body, on the physiological level, immediately translates any object or event "out there" through the senses into neural impulses "in here" within consciousness. Human consciousness, having a definite foundation in physical reality but being more than the sum of sensorineural activity, also immediately transforms and organizes these impulses into ideas, thoughts, and feelings that, in themselves, have no perfect external correlate. Even though all human consciousness is corporeal consciousness, consciousness itself cannot be traced back to any particular neuron. All the information about the external world passes through the body's limited sensory systems, which are themselves fine-tuned to perceive a limited amount of information. Concepts such as fact, truth, honor, loyalty, love, thread, tapestry, lens, bias, judgment, observation, deduction, data point, and nuance appear within the horizon of limitation.

Should a stimulus fail to meet the threshold potential of the associated neuron, the neuron does not fire and the signal does not pass along to the other neurons. The implication here is that some stimuli, although "real" as proven through animal physiology and scientific instrumentation, exist beyond our human physical ability to perceive them, and beyond our human body's physical ability to translate them into neurochemical signals, and therefore they remain unprocessed, unnoticed, and appear to be "not real" or absent. Our perception of a thing imposes our own limitations upon it, digesting it for our consumption so to speak, which makes it possible for us to recognize it as something in the first place.

Our perspective on the world is also limited to or is a function of our position in *space*. To illustrate this concept, suppose that a person walks through the door of a restaurant and pauses at its threshold. From their perspective, they might see various tables and chairs, waiting areas, waiters and waitresses hustling and bustling about, patrons standing or sitting immersed in various murmurs of conversation, and they might catch a whiff of various foods being shuffled in the distance, depending on the restaurant's design. The newest customer sees that some people are waiting nearby, while others are seated in the distance eating their meal. As the host or hostesses guides this standing patron to their table somewhere in the back, the customer's perspective changes. Each step toward their table enables them to occupy a different space along the route. The new ideas I present to you function in much the same manner as the customer's steps toward their table: each idea or step changes perspective.

During the walk to the customer's final eating location in the restaurant, the kitchen that was hidden from their view upon first entering now can be seen with various cooking instruments, ovens, fryers, griddles, chargrills, and range tops, all abuzz with heat and sizzle, with chefs and cooks preparing various appetizers, main dishes, and side dishes. From the door's threshold, although the customer could smell food cooking, their perspective limited them from seeing the kitchen. Only after passing by the kitchen on their walk to their table did the customer witness, understand, and appreciate the hard work that went into creating the wonderful aroma. Other customers, once obscured by the various décor at the main entrance, are now seen eating in different areas within the restaurant. Places within the restaurant, previously never thought to exist from the restaurant's threshold, show themselves as new areas to drink and dine.

Your journey with me began in much the same manner as the one perceiving the interior of the restaurant from the position of its threshold. At first, your general experience and intelligence prepared you for what you might encounter with me, e.g., you could smell the aroma of food cooking but did not know about the precise effort involved in order to produce the aroma. As I presented concepts for your consideration, you walked further into the restaurant with me and began to see new facets of its interior unseen from your previous point of view. In other words, wrestling with new ideas changed your position in space and considering new ideas allowed you to "move" inward and perceive new things—things not considered in such detail from your original position, such as the events happening in the kitchen.

Your limited perspective at the threshold might have led you to say something like, "I do not believe that a cup of water exists behind that wall." But after venturing forward into the restaurant and walking behind the wall, you saw the cup of water on a nearby table. Had you never stepped forward, had you never traveled with me or considered new ideas, you would have remained resolute in your assertion that the cup of water did not exist. If we build upon this idea further and introduce concepts such as love, discipline, the divine, righteousness, and spiritual resonance, you might again say from the threshold that "love does not exist," or "God does not exist," or "spiritual resonance" does not exist. To this, I answer "walk with me a little further and consider what I have to say."

Those who reject the idea of limitation add further evidence to its reality. In order to voice their opposition to this idea, they have to exclude other ideas contending for their limited attention. They must use certain words in a certain language to structure their rebuttal of the concept of "limitation" in order to produce their intended result. They might say, "I do not choose *limitation*, I choose *something else*," or "I do not choose all of *these ideas*; I choose all of *those ideas* instead," or "I choose not to make any choice at all," which was described earlier as still a choice made. Choosing one means excluding others; pursuing one means ignoring others. We perceive existence with our limits, through our limits, and because of our limits. Disagreeing with the limits from one idea means accepting the limits from another.

Similar to the perceptual limitations described as a function of space and as a function between human versus animal physiologies, there are also limits to intangible activities, such as thinking and feeling. Just as the body translates physical stimuli into neurochemical signals, one's perceptual lens translates and interprets meaning, relationships, thoughts, and feelings. One cannot perceive everything there is to be perceived or entertain every thought and feeling simultaneously because consciousness itself has limits. Instead, the individual lens, flawed as it is, enables people to understand and interpret a phenomenon within the lens's range or ability to do so, sequentially in *time*, which is another limit imposed on perception in addition to space. Other people might be capable of perceiving more or less, depending on their nature, intelligence, talent, and inclination to do so.

Most people exist being accustomed to and habituated with their perceptual limits, believing that "they see what is," just as the customer at the restaurant's threshold sees the restaurant's interior as a function of their position. However, while limits in the tangible space tend to hint that there is more available to see, for example, the size of the restaurant implies that there are other areas to be discovered; intangible limits rarely point to a means of expanding them, for example, perceiving the world with a certain lens does not immediately indicate a newer and better method of perception to replace the current one. But just as traversing space reveals new tangible things to the customer, entertaining new ideas and new ways of thinking and feeling reveals and influences new manners of perception through intangible means.

We know that humans share 99% of identical DNA with bonobo chimpanzees and common chimpanzees. The greatest works of art and literature, scientific discoveries, divine revelations, and all the achievements of the human race reside in the 1% difference between us and them. Researchers have discovered, however, that a few primates, such as the bonobo Kanzi and the gorilla Koko, have picked up using abstract sign language to communicate their thoughts to researchers in addition to them being able to understand hundreds, if not a few thousand, of spoken human words which were learned either directly or indirectly through exposure, similar to how human children learn the language of their parents. But even so, the abilities and general potentiality of human children outshine those of the most brilliant primate.

Anatomical differences between human and primate species in the vocal cords and in the tongue makes traditional speech easier for humans and more difficult for primates, while anatomical similarities in the brain and ear assist both with the acquisition and understanding of language. The similarities and differences in physiology alone between humans and primates influence the potential degree of understanding and the perception of reality that flows from a particular way of understanding. But that 1% difference between us and them reflects our greatest accomplishments, our cosmos, and the ability for us to know each other in a manner impossible for a primate to conceive.

Following astrophysicist Neil deGrasse Tyson's 1% imagination exercise,[15] imagine a species who is 1% different from humans in the same direction of the 1% difference between humans and chimpanzees and bonobos. To them, our greatest accomplishments and insights would appear at least mediocre and common or at most as similar to how the greatest primate accomplishments in the acquisition of language appear to humans. We cannot even begin to imagine how they would perceive and understand things due to not knowing how their tangible physiology creates the foundation for new intangible ideas. From our perspective, their rudimentary insights would never appear to our consciousness in

---

15   ThisIsRadioFreedom1. (2014, January 13). *Best explanation ever! To a fascinatingly disturbing thought! Dr. Neil DeGrasse Tyson.* [Video]. YouTube. https://www.youtube.com/watch?v=aTZyVZBtP70

the first place. From their perspective, the limits of our physiology simply express the reality we inhabit.

Between humans alone within our 1%, the number of neural connections differ between children and adults. As children learn over time, neurons in their brain both develop and produce more connections to surrounding neurons. Exposure to new information over time causes the brain to respond physiologically by creating new neural connections, *and* the processing and understanding of new concepts happens only after the brain forges new neural connections to do so. Observers should take note of the symbiotic relationship that exists between new ideas and physiology. Whereas the young child cannot grasp advanced mathematical constructs or abstract philosophical concepts like their adult counterparts do, children have the innate potential to do so one day, a potential actualized by and through the limits of time, ideas, and physiology. Surpluses or deficits among them will influence the perceptual lens through which objects in the world appear to consciousness.

Dear observer, let us synthesize our discussion thus far and alter our perceptual lens in light of the concepts described. It is time to see things anew and digest the food on the table of our couple. This thing called love and infatuation unfolding between man and woman is nothing more than a dance between two limited and instinctual animals who happen to walk upright. Each perceives the other through the tomb of the familiar. Any heat created from their sexual delight comes from the friction of using the other's physical intimacy as a tool for personal masturbation. Their intentions are to use one another as a means to an end, as an emotional Band-Aid, as a tool of convenience meant to warm the cold loneliness within themselves with emotions such as "love" and "passion." They are not interested in the evolution of their souls; if they were, we would see something different and more sophisticated. We might as well be observing a rooster chasing a hen as they too walk on two feet and are driven by instinct.

Because of the nature of limitation, everything a person is, does, or does not do is imbued with meaning and significance—you and I included. When a person chooses *this* rather than *that*, uses *this* word rather than *that* word, behaves in *this* manner but not in *that* manner, mates with *this* suitor but ignores *that* suitor, engages with members of the opposite sex using *these* rules but engages with some others using *those* rules, they are disclosing volumes of information about themselves to those able to see it. And I see it.

There is a reason why certain nuances appear in certain threads and not in others and why she is generous with herself with some, but selfish with herself with others. There is a reason why she is attracted to some and not to others, why she makes time for some and not for others, why she divides her heart one way for some but another way for others, and why she tells certain stories to some and not to others. She gives of herself to some while taking from others, denies some while accepting others, opens herself to some while closing herself to others. All action or inaction recorded from careful observation translates into another crumb, another data point. Remember them. Reflect upon the pattern they reveal, and ask yourself how their organization makes sense. *The assumption for us is that observed thoughts, feelings, and behaviors which, at first, seem to have no root in reason make sense from a certain point of view.*

CHAPTER TWO

>> ""
>
> *Women do not love men in the same*
> *way that men love women..*

FRACTIONS OF DESIRE

Remember that the human heart is legion[16] and the heart of a woman is no different. Like the rest of us, her individuality, her first perceptual lens, emerged against the background of her parent's union within a preexisting social context, value system, and moment in time. Her first ideas and thoughts were not her own but were handed to her from her social network of caregivers. Her internalized feelings of self-worth and validation depended on her mastery of other people's provisions. She was a "good girl" to the degree that she mirrored and embodied lessons from those in power in her personal environment and was a "bad girl" when she deviated from the path laid at her feet.

---

16 Mk. 5:9

She experienced her first bond with her parents within the context of pleasure, pain, and hunger. After her birth, both hunger pains and other physical discomforts provoked her to cry out to the world with her baby voice, instinctually beckoning her parents to render aid. Gradually, she learned to trust that her parents would appear shortly afterwards to provide her with some physical comfort for her physical pain. Distress, for her, faded after a changed diaper or after suckling at her mother's breast. She drank warm, sweet milk, overfilling her tiny belly, while resting against her mother's warm flesh, finding comfort in listening to the familiar pulse heard in the womb. Her position upon her mother's chest allowed her the opportunity to study her mother's adoring gaze, and she began to associate the pleasure from hunger's defeat with the one whom she saw. She began to trust, in a general sense, that acute pain eventually ends, that others will respond to her pain, and that she is not alone. Upon this foundation, she begins to build initial perceptions of the world.

But not all parents respond to the cries of their children with care and concern. There are some whose response is irregular, stressed, or devoid of warmth and compassion. She is not a little human being needing care but rather a thing making noise. Absent parents taught her that continued exposure to hunger pain and discomfort is a normal part of life, that she cannot depend on anyone else to help her in her hour of need, and that moments of comfort are few and far between at best and unpredictable and unreliable at worst. She learned to associate her continued physical pain with an empty room, a shrieking mother, and an aggressive or violent father. To her, emotional ambiguity and volatility, inconsistent care and concern, and inflicted discomfort following hunger's defeat were the norm. Instead of associating warm and compassionate faces who welcome her presence in the world with hunger satiation, she connects stern voices and faces contorted and annoyed by her existence with hunger's defeat, which sets the stage for her finding pleasure through pain and rejection. Upon this foundation, she begins to build initial perceptions of the world.

As she ages, she forms different bonds with different people through the lens of trust or mistrust and learns by trial and error that each person in her little world requires a unique form of interaction.[17] Schoolmates, relatives, family friends and acquaintances, teachers, brothers, sisters, and mother and father all form different bonds with her, and she responds in turn by forming different bonds with them. While certain thoughts, feelings, and behaviors remain consistent to more or less degree across her familial relationships, it is obvious that she interacts differently with her brother than with her mother, with her cousin than with her father, and with her aunt than with her grandmother. Each relationship is a unique expression, its own thread woven into her tapestry, and she quickly learns each person's set of idiosyncratic nuances in order to anticipate their reaction as a consequence of repeated exposure to them. She shows love and affection to them all, each in her own way, according to her ability to do so within the established familial value system. Each relationship constitutes its own microcosm imbued with a set of specific expectations and goals, parameters of what constitutes "appropriate" versus "inappropriate" behavior, and conditions of rewards and punishments. She learns who makes her feel good, who makes her feel bad, who is more likely to give her what she wants, and when to interact with others or when to keep away. She is a little observer, a child scientist in her own right. She gathers information from her environment and draws conclusions from personal experience. She makes deductions from observed behavior, imagines future responses, learns who dispenses pleasure and pain, and

---

17   Diana Davison. (2014, December 9). *The psycho-ology of women.* [Video]. YouTube. https://www.youtube.com/watch?v=mrwimK2vfeM

knows under what conditions each person demonstrates the behavior she anticipates.

She is a child. She is one person with many relationships—a miniature legion. Fractions of herself reveal themselves through each of her unique involvements with others, and she finds her voice across an interior landscape populated with others. She alone knows and controls how all her fractions, all of her threads, fit together in her tapestry. Over time, her mental and physical development shapes new and different bonds with others, both inside and outside her immediate family. Whereas young children of similar age play together one way, adolescents of similar age play with each other differently. The advent of womanly features now restricts the rough play between her brother and herself, an activity enjoyed during childhood once upon a time, and simultaneously makes for new areas of exploration between her and interested males. As physical changes in the brain between neurons create the possibility for apprehending more complex thoughts and ideas, the physical changes in her body also bring about new ways of interacting with others.

Widened hips, a narrow waist, and protruding breasts catch the attention of older men. For them, these are the two best visual indicators that signal reproductive fertility regardless of the female's chronological age. Evolution endowed her with wide hips to ease the baby's passage through the birth canal. Ample breasts show her physical ability to produce the milk necessary to provide the baby with nutrients. Her youth and beauty communicate health to older men; her clear, glowing skin and clear white sclera indicate a hospitable womb free from disease and sickness; her long, shiny hair silently reveals that she has been healthy for quite some time.[18] Lipstick upon her succulent lips calls forth imag-

18   Buss, D. M. (2016). *The evolution of desire: Strategies of human mating* (4th ed.). Basic Books.

ery of her vagina, and the blush upon her face artificially imitates blood filling capillaries during passionate moments. She presents herself as a sexual being amplified with makeup and finds the new attention from men simply intoxicating.

Evolution cares little for thoughts, feelings, social constructs, morals, the nuances in relationships, and perceptual lenses. Evolution primarily concerns itself with the propagation of the species, the casting of raw genetic material forward into the future for the continued survival of the species. Epiphenomena, such as thoughts, feelings, and behaviors, are useful to evolution insofar as they assist with mate selection and ensure the survival of children. Just as spiders are born knowing how to weave webs, bees are born knowing how to construct honeycombs, fish are born knowing how to swim in schools, birds are born knowing how to make nests, bear cubs are born knowing to stay close to mother, and trees are born knowing how to create leaves, the human female already knows how to attract a mate. And just as it takes time for creatures in the animal or insect kingdom to activate their innate instinct, the human female's mating selection strategies also do not pronounce themselves at first but rather at a certain point in her development, usually during adolescence. When her mating instinct activates, however, it will be through the lens of trust versus mistrust, within a specific value system, at a certain moment in time, with a person satisfying her instinctual rather than intellectual or emotional criteria.

Evolution has refined her limbic system over the course of millions of years to achieve the goal of securing a high-quality[19] mate able to provide her and her potential children with resources before, during, and after their birth. This is why newly activated females tend to gravitate

---

19   Essential Truth. (2018, January 10). *Jordan Peterson: Wimps, alphas & good men* [Video]. YouTube. https://www.youtube.com/watch?v=WvmlIZwunHE

toward certain males during adolescence. Athletic boys, muscular boys, tall boys, boys with wealthy parents, and boys with a high social status demonstrate the potency of their DNA. Adolescent human females will compete among themselves for high-quality male acceptance and attention through the limited means available at their disposal, which usually results in the vast majority of them granting easy mating access to certain males. Actors, singers, and models also showcase their DNA and their access to wealth and resources, which is why she indulges in mental fantasies with them and follows them on social media, decorates her room with their image, listens to their music, or watches them on television.

She ignores nerdy and geeky boys, socially awkward boys, and classmates with little to no access to wealth, resources, status, and power because they do not present an immediate benefit to her mating strategy. Ignoring those males with the greatest potential to become wealthy and empowered one day demonstrates her ability, or lack thereof, to discern the future and describes a value system revolving around immediate gratification. Female adolescent perceptual ability does not extend far into the future but rather is limited to the here and now. But time charges on. Later, not only will these "rejects" and "misfits" acquire wealth, power, and social status, but they will also earn the privilege of accessing the second-hand remains of her physical and emotional attention, long after she has worn herself thin from pursuing her first choice—the alphas.[20] Later in life, she intends to exploit the social trauma endured by the rejects and misfits by luring them with the promise of love and happiness, sex, female validation, and attention leftovers.

Her desire to associate herself with someone else's wealth, power, fame, and social status will lead her, inevitably, to investigate older males.

---

20   21 Studios. (2018, January 26). *Rollo Tomassi on why women are attracted to dominant alpha males*. [Video]. YouTube. https://www.youtube.com/watch?v=HTe0qNPT1hQ

Sometimes, these males will be a few years older than herself. Other times, many years will separate the two. High school freshman females often date high school senior males for a reason. High school senior females pursue males in college for a reason. High school females in the church's youth group are attracted to their twenty-something youth pastor for a reason. Enticing, seducing, and attracting an older male testifies to the power and gravitas of her feminine desirability and intoxication. He might be a loser in his own social circle, but to the naïve youth, he is a god and must be serviced as such, lest his attention wane. Security and validation for her mean performing intimate acts. There are numerous stories circulating among the youth about men in their twenties bedding adolescent females. Oral sex, anal sex, vaginal sex, heavy petting, deep kissing or a combination of all of the above describe their interaction together. Even though sexual behavior between people finding themselves on the opposite side of the age of consent is illegal in the United States, the fact that it keeps happening generation after generation means something, especially in the face of dire legal consequences. Men are attracted to a female's youth and fertility. Females are attracted to a man's status and power, which usually manifests as the man ages. Men want sex. Women want relationships. And the story of humanity is the telling of how men and women negotiate one for the other.

The transformation of her body during adolescence initiates a change in how males interact with her. When she was a little girl, it was appropriate for her to sit on her father's lap. Now that she is a young woman, it is inappropriate to do so, but it is acceptable for her to sit on a suitor's lap. Her brother's increased strength and height make it now inappropriate for him to wrestle with her like he once did when they were children, but play-wrestling with a suitor is fine. Childhood friends who once paid her no sexual attention look at her in a new light as they stammer over words and become awkward and shy in her presence and she in theirs. Strangers who once ignored her now acknowledge her sexual value with silent stares, whistles, or with outright dinner and date invitations, anything to be in her company and earn her attention. Being the ever-keen observer that she is, she notices the change from others and attempts to make sense of it. Discussions with female friends and advice from her mother, social media, books, blog and magazine articles, and television shows offer her a rudimentary interpretive framework and provide a reference for her to begin to understand her newfound power.

Throughout adolescence and early adulthood, various suitors express varying degrees of interest in her. Some catch her attention, others do not. Despite the differences in their height, weight, education, ethnicity, religion, wealth, taste in clothes and music, career choice, eye color, and physique, they all share the common desire to bed her or at least to obtain her friendship with the hope of becoming more than friends one day.[21] She *could* accept them all at once, but that would mean each would learn about the legion of others desiring the same thing. Such revelation must be avoided at all cost, lest a handful feel less special and abandon their quest in order to pursue someone who does make them feel special. Friendship, however, makes everyone feel special and she uses its siren's song to lure men closer to herself for safekeeping.

Should she feel the need to disclose the happenings of this relationship or that relationship, she will do so within boundaries designed to create agreement and consensus with the listener. She will reveal as much or as little information as she wants the listener to have in order to support the version that she wants them to know. She will leave out bits and pieces of detail concerning her personal involvement and contribution,

---

21   Coach Red Pill. (2019, June 29). *You can never be friends with a woman | CRP*. [Video]. YouTube. https://www.youtube.com/watch?v=iVcPjym1cyg

thoughts, feelings, and behaviors that she brought to the table, and will present the other person as the main character of the stories she tells. She will take on the role of passive recipient, the one to whom the action is done, not the one doing the action. She keeps self-incriminating secrets closest to her heart and defends them with another of evolution's genetic endowments: plausible deniability.

If all her past and present entanglements were to appear out in the open under the midday sun, with each man knowing about her relational nuances and intricacies with all others therein, how each man intertwined with others or stood apart according to her ends, and the unique value she endowed to each man, it would raise numerous consistency difficulties for her to answer. After knowing the ease in which other men have bedded her, some men might respond with bitterness that she subjected them to labors of mind and body more intense for weeks, months, and years before allowing them access to the same pleasure. "She made me work for an intimacy that she gave away so easily to others," they would remark. "She evaluated my character for months before granting the same access given to men after a few hours or days," others would observe. Still others might see themselves in contrast with those whom she actively pursued, when she demonstrated clear interest and intent, when she made herself readily available to pleasure them at a moment's notice with little to no effort needed on their part to initiate intimacy. They would question, "Why is it now my sole duty to arouse her and to chase her in order to make the smallest thing happen, her interest in me now far less than mine for her, when she once chased others with single-minded intent, with her interest in them exceeding their desire for her? What about them made it so easy for her to seek them out? What about me makes it now so difficult for her to seek me out? Am I now less than they or were they always more than me?"

Under the sun, all would bear witness to how she carried the nutrition, benefits, insights, resources, techniques, and conversations provided by one man within the bounds of one unique relationship into another man's domain for her to feast upon with him. Each would be able to see for themselves how one man plants the tree only for another to eat the fruit. The one investing is not the same who earns dividends from the investment. Her verbal expressions of gratitude to her provider translate into hugs and kisses for another. "Thank you" in recognition of his labor, effort, and utility means: "Thank you for making it easier for other men, not you, to have me, a benefit you will never know. Thank you for making it easier for me to love someone else, or rather, thank you for making it easier for somebody else to love me." She is not interested in rewarding the one providing; she rather takes from the first and rewards the second with the belief that her half-hearted reciprocal effort and simple acknowledgement matches the comfort and investment from the first. It does not and he should walk away and put her in his rearview mirror.

She is not required to, or expected to, reciprocate intimacy with the men who invest themselves into her well-being. His investment does not entitle him to intimacy from her. By the same token, men are not required, or are expected, to care about the happenings in her life. Her mere existence does not entitle her to attention, care, and concern. Should she cry out for help, no one is obligated to provide it to her inasmuch as when someone asks for a kiss or for some other token of vulnerability and affection, she, too, is not required to provide it. With that being said, she tends to fan the flames of intimacy in one relationship, enticing the man to give more of himself and his resources, but stops short of allowing him to reap any benefit beyond "friendship" with her. Her relationship with the first investing man is not reciprocal, it is parasitical. But rather than gorging herself upon the love, support, attachment, validation, and attention from her chosen partner, she involves herself with others and takes what she can from them, and brings their fruits to her partner's table and prepares the banquet of her body for him who did nothing aside from existing. For if he was sufficient in and of himself to her, she would never feel compelled to involve herself with others. But she does. She, in effect, denies most other men access to her in an attempt to virtue signal her devotion to her chosen partner. Select other men, to her, are but playthings and resources, unless of course, she chooses to entertain more than one "significant other" in secret or at least in secret to one of them. There are always exceptions to her rule. She defines the exceptions and she also defines the rules.

In essence, full disclosure of all her relationships, both past and present, to everyone involved in those relationships, both past and present, means that each person involved in them would finally see his placement along her hierarchical spectrum. Some seeing their place would feel that their higher rank placement is appropriate, if not altogether expected, while others would feel disempowered and unimportant because of their assigned lower rank. It would be apparent to all why she made particular men work harder than others for her affection, why she kept some men secret while parading others as a "best friend," why she required certain men to obey her rules while she broke them for others, or at least did not hold them to the same standard, why she chased some and refused to chase others, and why she smuggled the food grown with a man from one relationship in order to feed another man in another relationship. The men would begin to see that those among them possessing similar traits, features, qualities, or dispositions tend to cluster around others of the same within the hierarchy.

The most important reason motivating her to hide all her various relationships from communal revelation is the fear of abandonment. Once all men are able to see one another, one another's rank, and the commonalities each experienced as a result of his rank, they could then deduce the essence of her hierarchical spectrum, the guiding principle that binds together her system of evaluation. Not only would they know their placement within her emotional hierarchy, but they would also know the understanding that guided her to place them there in the first place. Her value system, and all the contradictions therein, would be transparent. Exposed by the midday sun, all her thoughts, actions, and behaviors with those assigned to a certain rank would be available for all, above and below, to inspect. No longer would she be able to insulate herself with secrets and mystery. No longer would she be able to collect trinkets of affection and store them in the museum of her heart.

She fears being exposed. She fears being abandoned. She fears that each man would see for himself that her power over them originates from their biological desire for her. She fears the possibility of having others know how she constructs and farms meaning and intimacy, and as a consequence, being placed herself on their hierarchical relationship spectrum in a place mirroring her rank and authenticity. They would do to her as she did to them; just as each man discovered that he was but one among many, they would place her in a hierarchy where she was also one among many. She would not be as special anymore—and this thought angers or saddens her. If all men were privy to their placement within her hierarchy, most if not all, would disappear and leave her to embrace one alone, the fool, and he would be the one for whom she settled, not the one whom she desired. "If he's the one you want, then you should have no further use for the benefits I provide," they would realize. "I would be a fool to accept so little in return for my investment.

Let the one you love more than me provide for you better than me," they would declare. "Let him alone protect you. My protection is superfluous and unrewarded. Let him alone teach you. My lessons are boring and unappreciated. Let him alone lead you. My leadership is insufficient and redundant. Let him alone feed you. My table is not comfortable enough and the emotional food I provide is not sweet or nourishing enough." Being truthful, forthright, and completely honest about all of her involvements is not in her interest, and she knows this, and such a revelation would unweave evolution's most potent gift to her: secrecy. In order to keep as many close to her as possible, she must make each feel special by speaking or doing the bonding language each man needs in order to keep his connection with her alive and well.

Piercing a woman's secrecy is like looking beyond the event horizon and perceiving the singularity itself. We can theorize about its existence, measure how it affects surrounding interstellar bodies, and reason out mathematical formulas matching the evidence collected. However, all of our greatest insights about her intentions are both limited and restricted to the instruments available at our disposal. Scientists use telescopes and we use observation and deduction. But the truth of the matter, at this point in time, is that seeing a woman's secrets is impossible or as equally possible as illuminating the singularity. For even if she volunteers full transparency, how does one measure its accuracy, for as our discussion thus far has shown, women tell the specific narrative they want you to know and believe. There is no definitive method and she too knows this. Therefore, trust must fill in what words and actions cannot. Either she will break it, bend it, or adhere to it. Is the juice worth the squeeze?

It is not in a woman's evolutionary interest to isolate herself to just one man. Even if she already has a partner, there's always a bigger and better deal out there somewhere. It is for this reason that she entertains friendships. Covert interaction with each of them alone at once avoids her potential exposure to communal shame and guilt and provides ample opportunity for her to wind the key in each of their backs. She converses with them all in a friendly manner, but remains superficial with some and not others, sends nude pictures and videos of herself masturbating to some and not others, and grants physical benefits to some and not others. She shows vulnerability and emotion with some and not others, shows defiance and aggression with some and not others, and cuddles some and not others. She knows that each suitor wants sexual intercourse with her, she knows that she alone controls which men have access to her and which men do not, and she also knows what to do or say to sustain the desire and interest of each one as each waits his turn to bed her. Women are the gatekeepers of sex[22] and men are the fools waiting outside the gate for admission.

She, like a herding dog, corrals her legion of suitors into the public "friendship" pin for everyone to see. She never hides her platonic relationships with these many different men. In fact, she believes that maintaining and sustaining various interactions with them testifies to her social virtue and desirability. After all, she must possess several endearing qualities that others find worthwhile to more or less degree in order to befriend so many. Because communal awareness of her carnal relationship with each of them would decrease the number of male friends on standby, she reasons that her legion exists for qualities beyond the physical as she does not openly share her body with any of them, and if she does, none know about the others. She will publicly testify to her chastity and monogamy and say things like, "It is easier for me to be friends with men than with

---

22   Coach Red Pill. (2019, September 1). *Women gatekeep sex—but men gatekeep relationships | CRP* [Video]. YouTube. https://www.youtube.com/watch?v=9LwJY8MWoLU

women." She is, after all, a selective and virtuous female, or so she tells herself. Should anyone inquire about her relationship with this man or that man, she would direct their attention with one finger extended from one outstretched arm to the friendship cage in the distance.[23] "He lives in that far-off cage and is nothing more and nothing less to me than one whom I call friend," she would retort. All her public interactions with each of her friends are civil and safe, and at times humorous, but never what an onlooker, especially another female, would consider inappropriate. Platonic evidence for each friendship is in the open for all to see. But observers are called to see the unseen, to bring light to darkness, and to find truth hidden in plain sight among deception. She is a female chameleon.

When a high-quality man expresses an interest in a certain sport such as hockey, baseball, basketball, soccer, or football, etc. to her, she will adapt to his taste and research the sport in order to find some way to attach herself to it as a proxy to attaching herself to him. When she implements this method of spontaneous adaptation, she is called a female chameleon because her strategy is to blend in with her surroundings. In this case, she wants to get closer to the man she desires, and therefore, she mimics qualities, attributes, and interests important to him. Her behavior is meant to lower his emotional defenses under the forced illusion of shared interests. She likes the foods he likes. She enjoys the same outdoor activities that he enjoys. Both listen to the same genre of music. Both are interested in traveling to distant lands. Her interests are a function of his interests and her dislikes mirror his dislikes. *Observers should interpret similarities between him and her as her nonverbal desire for an emotional connection with him. Focus on her legion and pay close*

---

23   Alexander Grace. (2017, November 2). *Orbiters - Interviewing university girls*. [Video]. YouTube. https://www.youtube.com/watch?v=HFA_U7X_Rzc

attention to the individuals she imitates. She endows such particular friends with a secret permission to access an intimacy not given to the others. Her rationale is that the more she adapts herself to him, the more that both he and she will have in common together and, in turn, the more attached he will feel to her. She constructed herself to reflect his tastes and desires, enabling her to anticipate his wants and needs before he even expresses them. If he wants intimate photos of her, she sends the intimate photos, even if it means her taking them in a bathroom mirror. If he feels lonely, she will comfort him. If he wants to knock upon her door, she will surely open it for him.

Smarter females will implement plausible deniability beforehand and will retort that they already had an interest in this sport or that sport or in this outdoor activity or that outdoor activity before he came along. In other words, they will deny that he inspired her fascination with this or that. She will say that their shared interests are therefore accidental or coincidental. It will be difficult to see beyond plausible deniability, to prove or disprove her statement unless it is somehow known that she is the one reminding him, subtly, of everything they have in common. But then again, she would consider such words a normal part of conversation and not a manipulation technique. Obfuscation and ambivalence make plausible deniability a powerful tool in her arsenal of attraction methods because implementing it allows her to perform an action or say a word without accepting responsibility for it unless it suits her need otherwise. When confronted about her plausible deniability, she will implement guilt and shaming tactics to remove the focus from her. She will say things like, "You don't trust me," "It sounds like you are insecure," or "Don't worry about him—we are just friends." It is important to remember that her plausible deniability allows her to live a double life, to entertain multiple contradicting emotions, and justify her behavior to the inquisitive observer.

General intelligence and aptitude, on the other hand, are not easily imitated. When her intelligence is lower than his, and she is interested in him and sees her lack of intelligence as a potential barrier to a closer bond, she will express interest in increasing her intelligence through independent means. She will investigate the books and ideas near and dear to his heart as well as discover works of literature that express her own individuality to discuss with him. Observers measure the authenticity of her action by measuring changes in her being in the world, not by what she knows but rather how she integrates her new knowledge with her stylistic presence to herself and others. Intelligence is measured by how one arranges facts and ideas to create a unique and cogent narrative, deriving something new from something common. The acquisition of intelligence transforms the person, motivating them to interpret the world in new and different ways. Intelligence feeds awareness and awareness is the catalyst for change. Fact gathering, on the other hand, sharpens her wit in one area alone, adding to the noise already in her echo chamber, but fact acquisition does not alter the general landscape and configuration of her mind and heart. She becomes a smarter version of herself, not a different version of herself. Pursuing knowledge for the sake of becoming a better chameleon versus pursuing wisdom to become a better human being, regardless of who notices, describes that her manner of seeking determines her manner of finding. Knowledge is nothing more than a means to an end. In this case, she acquires knowledge and fact to seduce a man more intelligent than herself. Once he lowers his defenses, she will sink her claws into him and drain him down to her level. She will entice him to play the game according to her rules and she will exploit his carnal desire for her. She will have the home field advantage and she will make him feel special during his surrender to her.

It is for this reason that more often than not, she pair-bonds with men less intelligent than herself. It is the path of least resistance. By doing so, she avoids the effort needed to improve herself, while at the same time she feels empowered against his contrast. As long as the dimwit remains well fed, so to speak, he is sedate and she can operate in the shadows without arousing his suspicion. He guarantees her security without question and believes that their frequent sexual intimacy reinforces the strength of their bond together. Unbeknownst to him, however, *females can give their bodies over to one man while simultaneously giving their hearts and minds over to others.* They can operate in two or more worlds or relationships at once without contradiction nagging at their mind and heart. The high school church girl surrenders her body to her high school boyfriend each night, but thinks about the spiritual, mental, and emotional bond between herself and her youth pastor. Both, to her, are safety nets meant to protect her from falling from the crib into dark loneliness. She will never describe the full intricacies happening in one relationship to the man in the other; however, her dual approach reveals the flaw woven into each thread as she leaves both doors open and walks through each door simultaneously: she will never be fully present in one relationship or the other, and therefore, any disappointment experienced in one divides across the number of her "friendship" involvements. What the man feels keenly, for example, $1 \div 1$, she feels little to nothing, for example, $1 \div 16$, or feels inasmuch as she is there with him, for example, 0.0625%, depending on the number of suitors hidden in plain sight in the friendship cage. The more suitors she has on the ready, the less she feels toward any one of them in particular.

The assumption for us is that observed thoughts, feelings, and behaviors which, at first, seem to have no root in reason make sense from a certain point of view. We begin by encountering her and her legion of suitor-friends. How must she situate herself in the world such that it makes sense for her to apply the "friends" label to this particular cluster of men and not to some other cluster with some other label? Did each of these individual men spontaneously appear from nothingness and by sheer accident wander into her presence whereupon she randomly and immediately bequeathed them with the title "friend"? I think not. All friendships have a beginning. All romantic interactions have a situational context, a narrative, or a story in which they appear. Microinteractions build into longer interactions. Longer interactions compound into distant involvements. And distant involvements pave the way for deeper entanglements. A few words spoken here and there during greeting and departing transform into longer sentences made to "feel each other out." Sentences become conversations and through multiple conversations, each begins to perceive and bond with the other.

If randomness were her guiding principle, it would indicate the absence of the evolutionary evaluation and filtering procedure meant to separate the dangerous and violent men from the safe and pleasant men. While it is indeed possible for her to befriend men with latent anger issues, evolution generally forbids building close ties with men who are immediately dangerous to life and health, lest some other mitigating factor interfere such as a chemical or a financial dependency, an organic brain deformation, a need to fulfill prophecies based in mistrust, a feeling of general unworthiness, a desire to reenact a childhood trauma as a means to either conquer it or be comforted by it, a desire for self-punishment, or a mythical belief in her ability to heal and change him. Regardless of the reason, each of her friendships always make sense from a certain point of view. Everyone carrying the public friendship title does so for a reason. Despite the many differences between the suitors, friendship with her is their common denominator. From this, the question that an observer should ask themselves is, "What is the ultimate object or aim, the telos, by which it makes sense for her to collect these particular men in this particular arrangement? What does each *do* for her?"

Let us start at the beginning and assume, at least for the moment, that she cares about her life and health and that her chosen friendships are also meant to further evolution's design. For anyone to be considered a friend at all in any sense of the word, there must have been a moment in time when she was a stranger to him and he to her. Every friendship starts somewhere. Once upon a time, interactions between them did not exist and from her perspective, he never stood out from other average, everyday people in the world. She, too, was a face among faces existing outside the scope of his awareness, at least from his point of view. Both he and she existed *per se*, in a physical sense, but they did not yet exist for each other.

Then something happened. The spark of creation ignited a big bang between them, and a new universe filled with potential was called forth from the dark and silent abyss of nothingness. Seeing the other, hearing about the other, or otherwise learning about the other manifested them into primordial existence. The manifestation of the possible simultaneously forged a new infant thread between them the width of spider silk; its placement within each tapestry making sense from the correct perspective. Threads strengthen between some and weaken between others as a function of mutual imagination and expectation, the exploration of nuance, and through projecting the new bond between themselves into a future of the possible. Imagination strengthens threads.

Imagination fills the distance between them. The other is as he or she imagines them to be; interactions between them are short and carry on through email, telephone, pictures or "selfies," or through text message. Missing is the constant face-to-face encounter with the other and the habitual ritual of being present during their ups and downs. Experiencing such things through artificial means enables imagination and yearning to take the place of bodily interactions in the flesh. Each reinterprets the other's "absence" as an "imagined-presence" in the realm of the intangible, and delusion soon replaces authentic presence. Over time, habitual delusion becomes their new reality and their new language. If they yearned for each other with so much intensity, then they should be together and leave everyone else alone. But perhaps he has a wife. She perhaps has a husband. Her thirst for attention and validation makes him like a drug she cannot or will not stop taking. And she, knowing how to entice his mind, provides him with intimate photos and intimate words designed to keep him on a leash. Their relationship, in essence, is nothing more than a time-proven opportunity to masturbate with either the idea or the image of the other. She gives this to him freely but expects others to earn the same privilege from her.

Friendships come into being and continue to exist because each not only throws the other into the future but also envisions themselves with the other in that future. For her, each male friend appears against the background of present and future opportunities according to her assessment of his unique arrangement of gifts and assets. Men find themselves within the boundaries of her friendship due to their social status, intellectual ability, humor, financial stability, physical endowments, abilities, or attributes, musical or artistic talents, income-earning potential, emotional availability, athletic ability, or because he reminds her of a previously encountered male now absent from her life.[24] Despite the countless reasons to keep the men in her orbit, it is certain that she keeps them there because they are useful to her in a thousand little ways. Each man fulfills a unique function to her as many others serve the same function; she tracks the longitude and latitude of each man sailing in her mind and heart and calculates their destiny with her long before they become fully aware.

Even though she converses with them all in a manner defined by the boundaries set forth within each thread, each relationship is its own universe, a reality unto itself, populated with its own unique nuances, expectations, thoughts, feelings, and behaviors. The naïve observer sees one woman with many friendships, but the experienced observer, on the other hand, sees the same woman replicated many times over across many relationships, with each replicant operating independently from the others.

Each replicant is both fully present to her current relationship and is fully aware of the collective consciousness of other replicants involved in other relationships. Contradictions do not exist for a particular replicant on the idiosyncratic level, as each operates according to the unique nuances, expectations, thoughts, feelings, and behaviors within a particular relationship. In contrast, contradictions emerging on the collective consciousness level between replicants are noted but ignored until proven useful for a particular replicant. The parameters of each unique relationship, not the original unifying female, determines the replicant's particular interpretation, understanding, perspective, role, status, and function within the relationship. This is the reason why she can change moods from one moment to the next, be a different version

24   Dr. Todd Grande. (2019, June 17). *Sexual economics theory vs. feminist theory | MGTOW, INCEL, & Science*. [Video]. YouTube. https://www.youtube.com/watch?v=M1R_pRxj9Zg

of herself from one relationship to the next, and entertain opposing ideas at the same time without much effort. She can be intimate with her body with one man, and be intimate with her mind and heart with another. She can communicate secret desires and yearnings to one man while sharing the same bed with another. She can appear in a certain light to one man and appear in a completely different light with another. She is legion.[25] Her friendships are legion. And her intimacies are legion. Whereas the casual observer sees one, the experienced observer sees many.

Her unique ability to fraction herself and endow each fraction with autonomy allows her to explore multiple possibilities simultaneously without feeling an overarching sense of guilt, shame, or remorse. There is no singular frame of reference within which to evaluate all relationships simultaneously. Rather, she evaluates multiple relationships using multiple independent frames of reference: one frame embodied within one replicant for each relationship. It would not be amiss to describe her condition akin to multiple personality disorder, but in this case, she is fully aware of all her personalities and determines the course of action each one takes. She is both the person standing in front and behind the mirror, herself and her replicant, and her shadow and its source. Depending on the context, relationship, and anticipated benefits, she can be neither, one, or all. Legion.

This talent allows her to ignore a man's existing commitments and relationships because from her perspective, the relationship she has with him has a life of its own and operates under the implicit or explicit parameters agreed upon by her and him. Since outside influences are not part of the agreement, they simply do not move her to care about them. If it is her intention to have sexual relations with a man otherwise spoken

---

25   Mk 5:1–13

for, she will do it, regardless of any expressed or understood commitment that either she or he already has. Sexual relations with him will happen whether or not he already has a child or is expecting his first child with someone else. Women have no problem intimately sharing a high-status male, i.e., someone in their group of friends desired by other females, a doctor, lawyer, politician, actor, or wealthy businessman, with his chosen significant other, usually without his mate's knowledge or consent of course. If she should ever cross paths with him again in public at some store in the future with his partner, and she with hers, she will approach him, greet him, and exchange pleasantries as if neither experienced such carnal intimacy with the other as their partners look on with ignorance.

She also takes no issue intimately involving herself anew with the same man at different points in time after prior relationships with him fell short. Being with the same man twice, three times, or more, regardless of the chronological time that has passed between reunions, shortcuts the necessary trivialities burdening the start of any relationship because this kind of relationship operates along qualitative time not quantitative time. They can "cut to the chase," so to speak, and "pick up right where they left off" because "it feels like yesterday" with each admitting that they have never really ever stopped thinking about the other. The passage of time, no matter how long or short, calls forth a new replicant which made the most recent reiteration of the relationship possible in the first place. If it were the same replicant as before, then the reasons for ending the previous engagement would be apparent and easily accessible and, with knowledge of the end, would prevent the most recent union from beginning. But a part of her believes, or fools herself into believing, that things will be different this time around. One replicant handled each of the prior versions. A new replicant handles the most recent reiteration.

Since replicants do not influence each other unless it is in her interest for them to do so, it becomes possible for her to ignore the lessons from past failures recorded in their collective consciousness. Unbeknownst to him, although she appears to be the same girl, he intertwines himself with a new replicant. When she finds it convenient to do so, her replicant feeds her imagination either with positive memories that justify being with him or with negative examples of past failures that justify leaving him again. Either way, as long as she likes him, she will either find or invent reasons to support her involvement with him. When she stops liking him, however, she will either find or invent other reasons to discontinue her involvement with equal emotion in the opposite direction. There will always be ample evidence to support whatever decision she makes. Facts do not stand on their own but rather stand upon the shoulders of their convenient emotional application. Feelings, not facts, guide the replicant's decisions.

Whether or not she actually physically involves herself with someone from the past is irrelevant. His continued existence as a person in her world speaks volumes about her motivation and intention. The fact that he appears to others as residing within the confines of her friendship cage is no accident. His appearance in this manner happens through her design and is meant to disarm suspicion. Keeping an ex-lover or an intimate friend around after their relationship ran its course serves to offer one more option, a known option, a backup option, should her current involvement fail or should an opportunity to rekindle arise. They may exchange pleasantries and idle chatter, talk about their current relationships with other people, and pass the time talking about hockey, soccer, hotdogs, race cars, politics, or old books. But the fact of the matter is that each has seen the other naked, exchanged pleasures of the mind and flesh, and have otherwise interacted in a very intimate manner together. To pretend that such a level of intimate remembrance cannot and does not influence their newfound friendship or their current involvements with others is ludicrous and delusional at best and insidious and underhanded at worst. Both he and she are one argument away with their current significant other from reliving the past, even if momentarily. The river of the past flows strong and hard underneath the land of the present. One needs but to dig in the correct place to access the latent water. *Observers must understand that her motivation is not to keep the past alive but to create the conditions of possibility for a future rendezvous.* In order for this opportunity to come about, her replicant must breathe life into his mouth from time to time to ensure his survival. This usually entails indulging in secret conversations and sending secret pictures in addition to their already public platonic demonstrations in person and on social media.

In order to ensure the secrecy of these interactions, she deletes the pictures of herself that she sends to him moments after taking them and sending them. Text conversations with him will also be deleted immediately, or at least the most incriminating parts of the dialogue. She does this so that if her partner asks to see her phone at random, she knows that he will find nothing that might place her in a negative light. Through removing bits and pieces of dialogue and pictures passing back and forth between them, she purposefully shapes the conclusions made by any inspector of her material.

On a side note, the invention of the smartphone created a new avenue for people to be private and intimate with one another. Before the advent of the smartphone, older generations wrote letters to one another, spoke with each other over the telephone, or they mailed Polaroid photos or sent greeting cards to one another. There was a certain premeditated intentionality to what they did. People back then invested time crafting written words to one another, and since corded telephones were, more often than not, located in public areas of the house, a private conversation was never guaranteed unless no one else was home for both parties. If someone was home, all they had to do was pick up the line in order to overhear the conversation in progress. The introduction of new technology, however, changed the communal consciousness and offered faster access to impulsivity and to immediate gratification. Secret messages and pictures can be deleted the moment after they are sent in order to maintain the platonic illusion. She takes her phone with her to the bathroom where privacy is guaranteed, shares pictures of herself in her bra and underwear to wind the key in his back, or she lays transfixed to the screen's eerie glow under her bed covers at night or after her partner falls asleep and texts about "what could be." She then deletes records of the messages and pictures and ensures that the other person does the same for the same reason.

She takes selective screenshots of private text conversations in order to store evidence that she may or may not use in the future or she copies and pastes his words into her notes program in order to remove the context that only she knows. She posts pictures of herself in the public domain on social media sites to ensure that the image of her face and body never leaves the mind of her community of "friends." Their responses communicate, in an indirect manner, their interest or acknowledgment. Her responses also communicate, indirectly, her interest and acknowledgment. When she likes his benign photos, she communicates that she is still thinking about him and wants him, in turn, to think of her—"I'm still here"—all of this with one heart emoji, a like, or a thumbs up.

Plausible deniability restates the fact that she cannot control how other people respond to her, that his photos are benign and her liking them means nothing, and that she likes many other photos, with his being one among the many. Why, then, does she check her phone so often, why is she so interested in *who* responds to her, and why is she so determined to provide responses herself? If others truly mean nothing, as she says, then why does she put in so much effort and time into an activity that means nothing?

If she had a long-distance intimate relationship in the past with a friend where they exchanged nude images of themselves, made frequent video calls showing themselves masturbating for the other to see, and either wrote or spoke lustful longings to be in the other's presence under the cover of night, her old replicant will maintain contact with him under the guise of platonic friendship if it is her desire to keep the old relationship alive to ensure a future possibility of encountering him. If it is her desire to keep her current relationship at the same time, then she will never reveal the full extent of the past relationship kept close to her heart after all these years. The replicant will find ways to entice the man from the previous relationship, the now "friend," during their time apart even as another replicant shares a bed with someone else. The operational parameters of her most recent involvement came into being well after she had established her role with someone else. Two replicants are involved here, one replicant for each relationship, each entangled in an existence separate from the other. Living out those old roles in the present means, for them, accepting the possibility that the other might find themselves romantically attached to someone else and then utterly ignoring it. Relations with other people have nothing to do with the relationship between them. Replicants do not mingle with one another as a general rule and find no contradiction in the face of contradiction.

Her youth minister, personal trainer, martial arts instructor, music teacher, gymnastics coach, coworker, physician, an old boyfriend or lover, or a current acquaintance might take a liking to her despite her intimate involvement with someone else. And for them, she creates a new replicant. In front of others, playful banter between moments of focused discipline disarms communal suspicion of their intimacy; however, the secret bond between them grows during moments alone together, whether that be time in each other's physical presence or virtual presence. Be it under the heading of a private lesson, a private conversation, an innocent status check-in, or a private meeting, she will make herself available to be alone with the men she likes, and she will make excuses never to be alone with the men she dislikes. She will not outright pursue him in a masculine way in order to maintain plausible deniability concerning her receptivity to his advancement. Instead, she will find a way to make herself available to be pursued. The burden of responsibility will be on his shoulders for pursuing relations with her, an already involved female. She will either reject his advancement in public or accept it in private.

Should the wrong man interpret her signal that it is okay to pursue relations, she will apologize and tell him that he misinterpreted what she meant. If she wants to keep him around for his usefulness or as a backup plan for later after his mistake, she will explain her behavior in terms of awkwardness, clumsiness, inattentiveness, or mindlessness. She might even say that her family treated her like a boy growing up and that she attributes much of her crude and crass behavior to their influence. Personal responsibility lies elsewhere, with her family, not with her. But should the right man of her choosing interpret her signal that it is okay to proceed, she will ask what took him so long to initiate and she will halt her masculine facade in order to showcase her feminine submission with an impish smile. She knows what men want. All women do. For the men she accepts, she submits to their desire without much hesitation. For the men she rejects, she turns into a blundering buffoon in a moment of convenience suddenly obtuse to male–female diplomacy. She either *confirms or denies* or *confirms and denies* her intention depending upon the observer.

Ambiguity is the language of plausible deniability. She will act and speak in such a manner that her behavior has no clear motivation or intent, but at the same time, drop breadcrumbs designed to put the burden of interpretation on the listener or viewer. This makes it safe for her to disavow personal responsibility for the breadcrumbs dropped. After assessing the various male responses to her stimuli, she picks and chooses which ones to keep and which ones to discard, depending on the narrative she wants each to have. For example, she will talk about her vagina, anus, or breasts in passing, describing some malady or discomfort in the affected area and leave it at that, leaving the listener to contemplate her specific bits and pieces. On a different day, her shirt rises as she stretches, exposing her soft abdominal skin and the top of her lacy black panties, leaving the observer to wonder whether or not she did that on purpose. Other times, she might want a hug or a quick shoulder massage and then momentarily grazes her breasts or thigh against the man's face, back, or arm, leaving the observer to think that she acted with intent and purpose, but has no way of proving or disproving it. She might wear a tight button-up shirt every now and then, drawing more attention to her large breasts, the freckled side of which can be seen between the buttons straining to remain together. If questioned, she might say that it is laundry day and that she has no other clothes to wear. Then there are those occasions when she warns not to stare at her ass as she walks away, which in effect calls attention to the forbidden sight. She might wear a short skirt or loose-fitting shorts without panties and sit in an oblivious position that grants a certain view to the perceptive eye from time to time. Meanwhile, she'll pretend not to notice the breeze upon her crotch as she sifts through her phone. When wearing blue jeans, she sits with one knee raised to her chest, spread outward a little farther than necessary increasing the space between her legs. She'll say that she's always sat in strange positions since childhood and that she did not mean to sit in such an inviting manner. When wearing tights or yoga pants, her thong underwear and shaven vaginal outline is plain to see. Calling attention to such a sight invites her to ask why the observer was looking there in the first place. Sometimes, she is caught staring with an expressionless face, seemingly hypnotized by some point on the man's body. She will not reveal what she was thinking about, but when pressed, will describe the narrative she wants the listener to know. She might make brief eye contact with the observer before licking peanut butter from a spoon or eating a banana. How else is she supposed to eat something other than putting it into her mouth? And then there are those situations when she speaks openly about the trials and tribulations of either past lesbian sex or current heterosexual intercourse with her partner. These are just stories, after all.

Under the guise of plausible deniability, her behaviors either are accidental and innocent or are meant to send nonverbal signals to a specific audience. Her words say one thing, her actions communicate another. Depending on who responds, either she will deny that her actions contain hidden motivation or she will welcome the attention. For every one of her behaviors, she has multiple explanations on the ready. The explanation she gives depends upon the one hearing it; the same action can be performed in front of two people, and she will provide each person with a different explanation. She will never accept personal responsibility and accountability for her actions unless it is in her interest to do so.[26]

Most warm-blooded men, upon seeing or hearing what she is putting out into the world over time, would interpret such actions and words as a persistent nonverbal communication of clear intent. Each one of her actions demonstrated tangible interest and when collected over time, communicates thematic information. Her use of intentional ambiguity throughout, however, translates into occasions for plausible deniability, empowering her to dispense the interpretation she wants others to have if directly questioned about it. Depending on the man who responds, she will explain her open disclosure and enticing behavior as a huge and embarrassing misunderstanding, as an indicator of a certain comfort level with him, as a function of her family's influence on her behavior that escapes her awareness, or as clear signals designed to be seen. *Observers should note that each of her friendships with men will likely contain degrees of sexualized behavior because she knows that implementing such behavior with them offers a quick, painless, and low-effort method for her to keep their interest as well as to gauge their desire and attraction to her.* This tactic allows her to catch fish without using a sophisticated net, so to speak.

Interactions within one fraction with one replicant do not contaminate or influence interactions occurring within another unless she believes that there is an advantage to their mingling together. For example, should a low-interest man express his sexual desire to her, she would excuse herself from him, citing unresolved issues stemming from an ex-boyfriend found in another fraction. On the other hand, should a high-interest man express the same desire to her, she would interpret

---

26   huMAN. (2020, August 26). *Women who want it ALL - hypergamy refuses to choose* [Video]. YouTube. https://www.youtube.com/watch?v=ohj6aIahX4Y

his interest as an opportunity to refuse to allow her ex-boyfriend from another fraction to keep her as a prisoner within this fraction. It is entirely possible for her to portray herself as emotionally damaged to some men while sending naked photos of herself that same night to other men. Her explanations for her erratic, distant, hurt, depressed, angry, or distrustful behavior given to some men do not inhibit her from being forthright, close, warm, compassionate, happy, and generous with others.

Dear observer, let us synthesize our discussion thus far and alter our perceptual lens in light of the concepts described. Just as new neural connections form in the brain, altering the physical reality of the brain itself, new methods of perceiving the world come into being as a result in the change in her physiology during puberty. A child's brain has the potential to understand the same advanced concepts held by the adult brain, with the chief difference being found in the density of neural connections between the two. It simply takes time and constant stimulus for new neural connections to form in the brain. Bodily changes in physiology follow a similar pattern and present new ramifications in both the individual and social domain, altering both the way in which she appraises herself and the way others evaluate her.

During infancy, she either learns to trust the world or to distrust it, depending on her parent's response to her hunger, and she carries these first successes or failures forward into the future where they later influence her adolescent mating strategies with classmates and older men. It would be to her evolutionary advantage to develop a strategy, whereby she can attract the greatest number of males while at the same time never committing to any one among them in order for her to explore the possibilities that each one offers. She might choose one from the many, but to pair-bond with one early on means excluding the potential from forming intimate bonds with others. Evolution dictates that she mates with the highest quality man available in her sphere, and the one whom she chooses may or may not be that man or he might be that man temporarily. Even if he turned out to be the best option among available options in the here and now, the future might reveal more and better options still.

The social convention known as "friendship" offers a path to achieve evolutionary mandates. Through it, she will be exposed to many potential suitors, will not be required to choose any one from their number, and will have them in close enough proximity to measure their abilities safely in order to determine which one offers her the greatest benefit. Insecure and distrustful women gather legions of male friends, otherwise known as prospective mating partners, over time under the guise of platonic involvement in order for others to see that she poses no detectable threat to the man's existing relationships. There is a reason why she makes friends easily and/or continues to keep alive friendships she had from a long time ago. Familiarity allows her to close the first act of the human mating ritual with each of them under friendship's label, keeping public suspicion low, with the first act being to collect as much information as possible about their suitability, as measured by their access to resources, income potential, wealth, controllability, genetic attributes, and social status.

It does not matter to her whether or not she already has a partner or that her "friend" already has a partner. She will test the waters with men who she perceives as having a higher sexual market value than her current mate before dropping innuendos and breadcrumbs of her intent while in his presence. This does not necessarily mean that she will leave one relationship for another. If she can maintain two or more relationships simultaneously, she will do so for as long as she reaps some kind of benefit from them, whether that benefit be money, attention, validation, or security. Women do not chase men the same way that men chase women; women make themselves available to be caught by men they deem worthy of her time and pleasure. For all the others, she will evade, make excuses, erect boundaries, and otherwise make herself unavailable to share private moments with them. If she is uninterested, she will enforce rules, play coy, confess a desire to remain chaste and follow acceptable social morality, always be occupied and busy, and virtue signal to others, in an exaggerated manner, her devotion to her current partner. If she is interested, she will not hesitate to break rules, defy social conventions, make exceptions, find the time, and make it obvious, both directly and indirectly, that she is attracted.

Most women do not show attraction or interest in a forthright manner because they weave plausible deniability into all their actions and inactions as a preemptive measure to protect themselves from potential inspection and scrutiny. With most if not all women, there is always a "good reason" for everything they do and then there is the "real reason"— the reason that they do not share.[27] They need to be able to produce an "escape plan" or a "narrative change" quickly should the situation arise, as would be the case when disarming a suspicious spouse asking her about her legion of male friends on social media. "Why do you have so many male friends," he asks. "They're not really friends, they're just acquaintances who sometimes post interesting things," she responds. By communicating this to her spouse, she placed emotional distance between herself and them. "Surely, she cannot have deep attachments or fantasies about people who are simply acquaintances," he reasons. He walks away. Her plan worked.

---

27   Sandman. (2017, November 22). *She has two minds - MGTOW* [Video]. YouTube. https://www.youtube.com/watch?v=jtktHMcDaV8

Because she anticipated that a confrontation might one day take place, as she knows that men tend to be territorial, she befriended a lot of different strangers and a lot of public entities who reflect nothing more than her interests as a means of creating her own public "white noise." She follows particular restaurants, intellectual or food topics, public figures, and music bands and likes their various social media posts. However, along with liking their public and benign posts, she also interacts with men "hidden in the background," that is, those men who have private profiles.[28] On first glance, these private profiles blend in with the white noise and her spouse will never see proof of her interaction with them. He will never see that she has been liking the same man's various public posts for years and will never pose the question to her, "Why have you been interacting with the same man for years, a man who lives hundreds of miles away, a man who you will never meet, a man who has nothing to do with our bills, our life, and our children? Why does it seem that you are involved so much with his life? Why are you keeping track of the happenings of his life? Why are you so interested? What kind of connection must you have with this man such that you invest yourself into knowing him?" She would respond, "He's just a friend I met a long time ago"—this is the "good reason" I mentioned earlier.

The "real reason" is that she has an emotional attachment with this long-distance man, and that their social media interaction together is made to enhance the platonic proof of their limited involvement. "He is in the friendship cage," she says. She will never reveal that she continues to send him text messages and images of herself in private and that she "winds the key in his back" from far away with an impish grin. She will never disclose her real feelings toward him to her spouse and risk rocking

---

28   Red Pilled Rican. (2019, December 29). *You need a zero tolerance policy for her male "friends"; aka: Beta orbiters*. [Video]. YouTube. https://www.youtube.com/watch?v=bautHAWm5As

the boat in her current relationship. She cannot disclose that when she closes her eyes during intimacy, she is really thinking about the other.

Regardless of the "good reason" or the "real reason," there is a reason that she is always on her phone. She is drinking the attention provided by her legion of orbiters;[29] with plausible deniability, she will say that she is checking on family members or that she is reading up on the latest book, musical debut, or design idea. While that might be true, such an explanation does not describe her need to post selfies or personal information about herself for the world to see. Who are her personal images meant for and why make any photo at all available for public inspection? I speculate that she places images of herself out there into the ether with the hope that she reaches one or a few intended targets. Because her photos exist in the public domain, she can say, with plausible deniability, that her photos are meant for no one in particular. At the end of the day, however, there is no real way to filter out the truth from the deceit. For this reason, information collection should take into account surrounding circumstances and her patterns of behavior over time. But the female chameleon is always one step ahead. Knowing that her behavior is available for observation means that she will act in a certain manner on purpose, over time, to establish a plausible alibi. She knows that if she presents herself in a certain manner in front of certain people with a degree of consistency that others will begin to see and believe what she wants them to see and believe. The best liars are the ones who pronounce their inability to lie.

In order to resolve the apparent conflict between remaining in a committed relationship while evaluating the worth of potential mates, she fractions and replicates her consciousness into multiple alternative

---

29   Sandman. (2015, June 13). *Beta male orbiters - MGTOW*. [Video]. YouTube. https://www.youtube.com/watch?v=R7q4i2_OWn8

versions of herself known as replicants. Whereas most people evaluate information in the environment from a single point of reference, the self, replicants differ in that each operates as an autonomous unit interacting within the parameters defined in each relationship. Friend *A* interacts with replicant *A*. Friend *B* interacts with replicant *B*, and so forth. The mutually agreed-upon rules, roles, interactions, parameters, expectations, understandings, and interpretations occurring in *A* do not apply to *B* unless deemed convenient to her. For example, if she feels that the situation in relationship *A* is getting out of hand, she will borrow information learned from relationship *B* in order to achieve her purpose in relationship *A*. This brief exchange does not influence relationship *C* or any other relationship.

She creates as many replicants as she has friends, which allows her to explore each friendship, each "fri-lation-ship" as it were, independently and simultaneously. This is how she is able to make herself available for sexual relations with a man otherwise committed to an existing relationship with her full awareness and consent. She simply does not care as it is natural for multiple women to share a high-quality man among themselves. Just think about the number of adolescent females throwing themselves at the high school football quarterback. Each female knew about the others but did not care; the attention he paid to one increased her status, even if temporarily, before he moved along to the next female the following week. Each of them hoped to lock him down with their feminine talent, not expecting to be discarded in light of many options.

His partner remains outside the scope of the replicant's involvement with him and therefore his partner does not exist to the replicant. The replicant does not believe that the promises and vows sworn with his current partner apply to his particular experience with her. The replicant is aware that he already has a partner, ignores it, and goes about her business with him. She disregards any thoughts and feelings that his partner might have if she were to discover their secret copulation. He will not tell. The replicant will not tell. It will be their secret and his partner will never taste the replicant on her lips. If she herself is involved in a relationship with C, then the actions done within A or B do not influence C unless she perceives a benefit from their mingling. But even then, she will never describe all the intricacies and nuances from either A or B to C—only those specific details that help her with her goal within C.

Do you see, dear observer, how she spends her time chasing the wind, implementing this strategy or that strategy under the cover of secret and deceit? Manipulation[30] and seduction have been teaching her about the world since adolescence, as no others have proven reliable. She draws a false sense of power and comfort from her legion, believing that she authors her own fate, never contemplating the hunger in her heart, never realizing that her quest for acceptance and security originates from pain, suffering, and abandonment.

The ones who were supposed to love her unconditionally did not. The ones who were supposed to guide her development criticized her, punished her, and left her alone in a silent room inside her infant crib to face the darkness alone. She was spanked too much as a child. She was handled too roughly as a child. Her mother screamed and shrieked at her too much as a child. She witnessed her brother falling at the feet of her father before falling herself from a single strike from his hand. She was raised and trained as an animal. The baby inside her cries from hunger pain even to this day, but all who respond to her are men with sexual intent. Any attention is better than no attention at all, so she surrenders

---

30   Thinking-Ape. (2013, December 7). *Biology, the female and manipulation.* [Video]. YouTube. https://www.youtube.com/watch?v=XzOJW1noHfk

herself to them, hoping that *this one* will lead her to the light. She at once loves the attention from men and hates it, for she never really knows if someone new cherishes her based upon her own merit as a soul in the world or as a means to an orgasmic end. She is doing the best she knows how within her means.

For these reasons, she fumbles from one relationship to the next, searching for the father she never knew, hoping to find the comfort never experienced as an infant sleeping upon his chest. Her attention and validation-seeking behavior, in all its manifestations, is born from the hunger within. Both her male friends and the men whom she beds reflect the weaving together of her evolutionary instinct and her childhood mistrust. Upon this foundation, she has built perceptions of the world.

CHAPTER THREE

> **"**
>
> *Be fruitful, multiply, fill the earth and*
> *subdue it.*
>
> —*Genesis 1:28*

FRACTIONS OF PURPOSE

Being human is a choice and all choices limit themselves to the horizon within which they appear. We cannot choose not to choose, for that too is a choice. We also cannot choose to stop being ourselves in order to adopt the personhood of another and begin living their lives in their place as if we were them. The flesh, consciousness, and essence from one person cannot replace another's with the expectation of being the same, even when both individuals share the same DNA, as is the case with identical twins. Differences in personality, feeling, thinking, and behaving will pronounce themselves against a background of identical genetic material. For as many similarities as there are between people, there are an equal number of differences, even if those differences remain hidden in the beginning.

A human being cannot choose to become a rock, for example, as the rockness of the rock, that which makes a thing as it is and not something else, is not within the human being's nature. We all know, intuitively, that rock nature is not human nature and that neither possesses a nature to assume the other. We can imitate a rock, however, and color our skin to appear as a rock, and withdraw into ourselves to replicate, in close approximation to catatonia, the silence of a rock. But we cannot strip ourselves of our humanness and adopt the being of a rock while maintaining the same level of awareness that tells us that we changed from one thing into another. To the best of our knowledge, rocks and humans are radically different from one another, despite both inhabiting physical reality with atoms, molecules, and stardust. Both might even share a few of the same natural elements on the periodic table, with more or less concentration depending on the particular rock, but a few similarities in one domain should not be interpreted as total similarity across all domains.

Our nature is to be human and nothing else and other things in the world are meant to be themselves and not anything else. We do not experience radical and spontaneous transformations of one thing into another, like human to rock, leaf to star, or kitten to volcano. Rather we experience objects and things through their stability over time and base our confidence in our perceptions upon such. We can, however, endow nonhumans with human qualities, a procedure known as anthropomorphism. Seeing some aspect of our own human behavior elsewhere in creation is not seeing the thing as it is from itself through itself but seeing the thing and comparing the thing to experienced human behavior from itself through our interpretation of it. It is we who attribute our behavior to them, seeing our behavior in them, not the thing who sees their behavior in us. For example, we might describe an angry storm, a soothing breeze, or say that fish swim away from sharks with fear, or that our domesticated pets love us. And while there might be some emotional elements shared between humans and nonhumans, it would be a grave error to think that nonhumans are in fact other incarnations of humans due to a few overlapping similarities.

Only other humans such as ourselves bind to and move within human horizons. Angels and demons, whether fictitious or not, cannot be humans, even though their nature and ours share a few qualities, such as thoughts, emotions, personality, and comprehension, like how humans and rocks share a few similar attributes and material aspects. The differences, not the similarities, between two things allow us to perceive each thing independently. If all things in creation were in fact so similar to one another that no difference could be detected, then we could not perceive at all because there would be no difference between us the perceiver and the objects we perceive. Understanding appears in light of the contrast between things, enabling us to see the uniqueness of them. Expanding horizons is our task as observers, but in order to travel to new lands with new horizons, we must first have an understanding of our current surroundings.

All knowledge is human knowledge. All wisdom is human wisdom. Even if one believes that they are the mouthpiece for heaven or hell or for some other spiritual plane of existence, for us, as humans, to be aware of such profound divine revelation, it must translate and "reduce down" into human awareness. The Bible, believed to be God's revelation to humanity, was written and translated with a human hand that was guided by God's Spirit, as scholars teach, into human dialect. Humans wrote their oral tradition in Hebrew for the Pentateuch, in Greek for the Septuagint, in Latin for the Vulgate, and in Old English for King James. The concepts therein, divine in nature, use humanity's apprehension of them as a vehicle to announce themselves to the larger community. As the world we see with our eyes translates into neurochemical signals sent to the brain, which in turn, processes these signals into personal ideas which then are evaluated against the backdrop of other ideas and experiences, everything divine and "otherworldly" we are able to grasp for understanding must first pass through our human lens in order for such things to come into focus for us. This works in both directions.

As humans interpret the divine through a human lens, the divine often presents itself to humanity in a manner that humans can perceive. The faithful believe that God once appeared as a pillar of fire,[31] a burning bush,[32] and through many other signs and wonders in ancient Egypt. God did not appear as Himself from Himself to humans, but rather translated and manifested Himself into things and acts perceptible to the human intellect. When He acted, and when we perceived Him acting as such, He did so in a manner intelligible to humans, for example, He appeared as a whisper in the mountain to Elijah,[33] He parted the Red Sea for thousands to witness,[34] He turned the waters of the Nile into blood,[35] and He also reclaimed the first born.[36] What He says and does in heaven is beyond the scope of our limited nature to perceive with clarity, therefore, we feel alone, small, and insignificant beholding the great chasm separating us from Him. However, those with certain gifts of the Spirit are able to perceive more because He endowed them with a gift, specifically allowing them to see more.[37] Even so, it is also said that even the highest angels

---

31   Ex. 13:21-22

32   Ex 3:2

33   1 Kgs. 19:11-13

34   Ex. 14:21

35   Ex. 7:21

36   Ex. 11:5

37   Jl. 2:28

dare not look upon His face lest His radiance obliterate their existence. These angels, anthropomorphized, shield both their "bodies" and "eyes" with their "wings" when "standing" in His raw presence.[38] Only the Son sees the Father iris to iris, as Dante observes.[39]

Horror movies and works of human imagination would have us believe that demons and various other evils manifest themselves from themselves unto our plane of existence to inflict all sorts of trials and tribulations upon man. But nothing happens among them without either God's permission or God's awareness, as is written in the Book of Job. If demonic intentions went uninterrupted and unchecked from the start, then the human race would have been their food long ago. Evil in our world is not found in pure spirit, but in the flesh, through the flesh, perceived with our flesh, embodied in this person or malady or that person or malady across history. Good and evil require human collaborators and participants, some physical counterpart, to manifest unto our plane of existence.

There are rules and restrictions in place dictating that any divine interaction with humans be done in a human manner and be perceptible on some level to humans. God "walked" with Adam in Eden;[40] Adam did not walk with God in Heaven. Whether or not you, fellow observer, personally believe in God or in things divine is neither relevant nor the issue at hand. This discussion is meant to communicate that there are limitations or parameters to the reality we inhabit and that our apprehension of the most important divine things occurs through our flesh and through the limitations of our intellect, emotions, and spirit. I have

---

38   Is. 6:2

39   Alighieri, D. (2003). *The divine comedy (The inferno, the purgatorio, and the paradiso)* (Illustrated ed.). Berkley.

40   Gn. 3:8

taken an extreme example of "not human reality"—the divine—and observe that the extravagant and important concepts therein manifest themselves within human reality. How else are we to speak about such matters? Divine things, objects, or ideas located outside human apprehension are, by definition, imperceptible to humans similar to how visual information outside the eye's ability is hidden.

Humans can spend a lifetime chasing clarity of the divine, something held most precious for billions, and its fruitfulness will still fall short, even after the Father beckons them to seek, ask, and knock with and through gifts divine.[41] If we cannot perceive that which we hold most dear using our own faculties, except with divine assistance, or at most perceive it imperfectly using our fallen senses, how can anyone claim to see lesser things with greater clarity, such as the fruit between man and woman?

Freedom and choice have limits similar to how seeing and hearing have limits. We cannot choose to transcend the threshold of human limitations, such as choosing to change our eye color or height through an act of will, nor can we choose to be aware of something dwelling outside of our awareness whether that awareness be implicit or explicit without some kind of prior microscopic awareness beckoning us toward it. We must perceive at least the smallest shadow molecule of a thing within our limitations in order to have some kind of awareness of it. We cannot choose to become something other than ourselves, like a rock or an angel, because our inherent nature limits, restricts, and allows us to "open up" on our plane of existence. We cannot see, hear, touch, taste, or smell beyond the limitations of our five senses because we would have no referential frame within which to process and interpret the new

---

41   Rom. 3:23; Jn. 6:44; Lk. 11:9; 1 Cor. 12:1-11

information. And we cannot begin to perceive thoughts and ideas that dwell outside our scope of us perceiving them in the first place because we would not be equipped to understand and recognize them as such. While "outside" things exist for some, they are hidden from others, similar to how some are able to grasp complex mathematical truths while others cannot. "Outside" unavailability to a few does not mean universal unavailability to all. Each perceives according to their nature and their limits. All human beings perceive through their limits, with their limits, and because of their limits.

Matters of the heart and mind occur along the same understanding. To the one born into confusion, into distrust, into pain and suffering, and into neglect and darkness, experiences such as love, comfort, understanding, empathy, and connectedness appear foreign and distorted. For them, tasting new positive emotions is like tasting various wines without cleansing the palate between each new glass. Blemishes in their lens skew and mutate their interpretation of positive emotions and experiences. They are not in the habit of cleansing their palate or of understanding how their blemish influences their perception; seldom have they experienced positive things as something positive before. The appearance and apprehension of such things is a function of their overall clarity or ambiguity. For them, matters of the heart and mind come into focus after passing through blemishes in their lens, meaning that what appears to consciousness is a new thing that is the combination of what is being perceived and the particular manner of perceiving it, for example, if one looks at something commonly accepted and described as "yellow" through their personal "blue" lens, it will appear "green" to their consciousness. Experiencing "greenness" does not lead them to question the "yellowness" or "blueness" of the thing because it appears "green." Similarly, if "love" passes through the lens of "mistrust," then one experiences "mistrusting-love," if "compassion" passes through "pain and suffering," then one experiences "suspicion," and if "empathetic understanding" passes through "neglect and darkness," then one experiences "malicious intent."

Experience carves out their presence in the world, announcing itself to others, revealing a particular situatedness or attunement. From their perspective, yellow things in the world appear green. Experience also shapes the perceptual lens by which other objects and ideas in the world come into focus for them, for example, green gradually overtakes blue. Experience at once guides their particular manner of understanding and the lens that makes objects available to consciousness for them to understand in the first place, for example, what was once blue grows greener, and therefore, all various colors in the world skew closer to green, each in their own manner according to their own color.

Without choosing something different and putting forth the willful and concentrated effort into breaking the cycle, experiences form a positive feedback loop within consciousness, coloring both what they know and how they know it, for example, green compounds upon green. People see what they see as they have been conditioned to see it without awareness of the conditioning; consciousness perceives objects of consciousness through a blemished lens without understanding the influence that the blemish has upon that which is perceived. But all of us perceive through our blemishes, with our blemishes, and because of our blemishes, therefore we must always be vigilant and continually strive toward clarity.

Let us adopt the language and insights of cellular biology to sharpen this point. Selective permeability refers to the deciphering activity of cellular membranes which allows certain molecules inside the membrane while expelling waste and other material to the outside of the membrane.

The cell "knows," inherently through chemical identification, which materials constitute nutrients and which materials constitute waste. If cells did not implement selective permeability, they would surely die,[42] mistaking waste and toxins for nutrients and mislabeling nutrients as waste to be expelled. In a similar manner, one's perceptual lens mimics selective permeability, and blemishes in the lens have the potential to misidentify nutrients from others as toxins or to mistake toxins from others as nutrients meant to sustain spiritual psychological, emotional, and intellectual life.

From their point of view, love and passion from the outside pass through the blemished lens of suffering and despair before reaching their interior world. Touch and compassion from the outside pass through neglect. Truth, knowledge, and wisdom from the outside pass through abandonment, nihilism, and skepticism. Happiness, pleasure, and anticipation from the outside come into focus through mistrust and anger. In a similar vein, thoughts, feelings, and behaviors from the inside also pass through these blemishes before manifesting themselves to others on the outside. Oftentimes, people do not use clear and concise words to identify their correlating feelings or thoughts, a misunderstanding reinforced through an internal mislabeling, or they use the same word to describe many different thoughts and feelings. Either way, imprecise language fuels deeper misunderstanding. If one uses words that incorrectly identify a thing, how can they expect their listener to know what is being talked about?

It is no wonder that proper communication between humans is so difficult and complex a task, with words and meaning passing through blemishes to and fro between them, compounding and straying further

---

42   Gn. 2:17

from clarity with every new sentence, which are in turn, embedded in prior blemished exchanges. People often "speak past one another," misconstruing the other's meaning and intent, or "see something that is not even there." They spend much of the conversation deciphering the meaning of words, agreeing or disagreeing with one another about the ideas discussed, and contextualizing implications within the scope of personal biases, blemishes, and preconceptions. Many discussions of this sort serve as a self-fulfilling prophecy, as an opportunity to showcase what one already assumes rather than as a means to expand internal horizons with another person's wisdom and insight.

How, then, does one change and bear fruit?

We begin with Aristotle's first sentence in Book I of his *Metaphysics*,[43] "All men by nature desire to know." The pivot word in this sentence is "desire," with the implication that desire and knowing are somehow woven into the fabric of what it means to be human, that desiring precedes knowing, and that knowing comes about after desiring. Let's take a closer look at the meaning holding the words together. While possible in a fallen, forsaken, or self-reflecting application, desire is not meant to be an end in itself, an empty activity that delights in its own presence, but instead requires an object outside of itself, "knowing," to pursue in order to actualize its purpose. A certain intentionality, a certain "for the sake of which," is bound up with the desiring activity and is needed, beforehand, to guide the activity, i.e., "desiring for the sake of knowing," means that knowing calls forth desire as a tool for the object of knowing to be known. The fruit of knowledge, what one imagines will be gained through the endeavor of knowing, the telos or final cause, exists first in the imagination and then beckons concrete desire to bring it about. "To

---

43   Aristotle. (1999). *The metaphysics* (New ed.). Penguin Classics. (Aristot. Met. 1.980a).

know" also implies that there are objects or things to be known; knowing implies a deeper reaching toward something beyond itself, for example, knowing is not a self-reflective endeavor meant to ponder itself in order to reveal itself. Instead, knowing is meant to reach and grasp concepts that are out of reach, a kind of stretching beyond itself to know something situated in the what, when, who, how, and why outside of itself; knowing is always about a knowing of something; the objects and fruits of knowing are out there waiting to be discovered but are as of yet not discovered, and the required vehicle to travel from unknowing to knowing or from less knowing to more knowing, or from one kind of knowing to another kind of knowing, is desire.

In the New Testament, Jesus taught that seeking, asking, and knocking were necessary preconditions to bring about finding, receiving, and door opening.[44] Both Aristotle and Jesus taught that certain actions produce certain consequences—desiring knowledge leads to acquiring knowledge, seeking leads to finding, asking leads to receiving, and knocking leads to doors opening. The teaching of Jesus clarifies, in a concrete way, the divine's role within the human equation: that some kind of human movement toward the divine always occurs first and that the divine's response always occurs second, even if that response is silence. Of course, this understanding does not imply that the divine grants absurdities outside the scope of its will, such as there mere act of seeking a hidden box of coins in the mountain from a dream always leads to one finding them when awake, asking for the sun to leave its place in the sky to dance around the heavens on a whim always makes the event happen, or that one is meant to knock on every door in existence, no matter how forbidden. Nor does this understanding contradict the essence of 1 Jn.

---

44 Mt. 7:7

4:19, "We love because he first loved us," because from the Christian perspective, the divine defined the rules of the formula long before the first human implemented it. One of the formula's operant conditions is the requirement that humans initiate the "ask–receive / seek–find / knock–open" relationship and that the divine *always* responds. He never said, "Seek and you will find ... *sometimes,* or ask and you will receive ... *on occasion,* or knock and the door will be opened ... *when I feel like it.*" On the contrary, He said, "For everyone who asks receives; the one who seeks finds; and to the one who knocks, the door will be opened"[45] with the understanding that the response, no matter how great or small, will always be for a person's greater good,[46] even if silence is needed to bring about that greater good.

The divine assumes the submissive role on purpose, despite all its might and power to eradicate the universe, keeping revelation to itself until stirred by human desire or its own will. There are many occasions in the gospels where the people, not Jesus, beseeched the performance of a miracle either on behalf of themselves or on behalf of another person or group of people. It is often written that after the miracle performance, Jesus cited or acknowledged the person's faith in Him as the primary motivator for His involvement, as the necessary antecedent cause to the consequential miracle performance. Mary, mother of Jesus, first moved Him at the wedding at Cana,[47] the official sought out and approached Him to heal his son,[48] the evil spirit in the man provoked Him,[49] the

---

45   Mt. 7:8

46   Mt. 7:9-10

47   Jn. 2:1-12

48   Jn 4:43-54

49   Lk. 4:31-36

man with leprosy asked Him to be made clean,[50] the centurion asked for his servant to be healed,[51] four men carried a paralyzed man to Jesus for healing,[52] and so forth. Even those miracles performed not due to individual provocation were conducted to benefit a human audience such as feeding the multitudes with fish and loaves[53] and witnessing the transfiguration.[54] The miracles of Christ always involved other people in some form or fashion.

The divine positioned itself long ago to respond to humanity's desire and movement, if not for a particular person or a specific group of people, then as an available and willing resource for humanity in general. The purpose of recounting stories from the Christian tradition is not meant to impose one religion upon another but rather is meant to describe the relationship between humans and the highest and greatest order presence that humans have ever encountered, God, a Being that is precisely everything we are not: omniscient, omnipresent, and omnipotent—a Being, too, that stands apart and outside human limitations, such as time, yet must pass through our five senses for us to comprehend His lessons, as was His design.

Desiring, seeking, asking, and knocking for its own sake, without expanding purpose or intentionality, is an empty activity that comforts with the illusion of motion, like the spinning of a merry-go-round, no matter how fast or slow, with no real distance traveled from one point to another, always mistaking its own "vibrating" as movement within the confines of its own limits. Any movement generated is but a movement

50   Mt. 8:2

51   Mt. 8:8

52   Mk. 2:5

53   Mk. 6:43

54   Mt. 17:1-8

from itself *upon* itself *toward* itself and produces no reward *beyond* itself. However, seeking, asking, and knocking with an intention outside themselves are guided beforehand by that which is sought, asked for, and that which lies behind the door knocked upon. The desire for something both manifests itself in and finds purpose in its intentional object, the goal, telos, or final cause of the desire, of the seeking, of the asking, and of the knocking. For desiring, seeking, asking, and knocking to be fruitful, they must reach or stretch out beyond themselves to their intentional object.

If we accept that desiring, seeking, asking, and knocking are guided beforehand by their particular intentional object, the implication is that the one doing the action is or was always-already aware, at least on some faint, shadowy primordial level, of their inspirational object. However, given that limitation both restricts and enables awareness within a certain range within either physical or mental realities, either new intentional objects already exist within the boundaries of limitation at the beginning, remaining latent, hidden, and undiscovered, that is, one's potential to transcend their limitations is built into the structure of limitation itself, like a tunnel long hidden inside the perimeter of one's mind which leads to a new land, or that perceived limitations are themselves imbued with a certain permeability, allowing individuals to apprehend things just above or just below the threshold of awareness, *meaning that one's ability to perceive their own limitations is itself limited.* Whichever the case, experience shows that some people *do* change, meaning that some people *can* change. Experience also shows that some people *do not* change, meaning that some people either are *unwilling* to change or are otherwise unable to do so.

The difference between changing and repeating the same depends upon the presence or absence of desire and the particular intentional object of desire. When one uncovers a hidden tunnel leading to change already existing within, so to speak, the implication is that one was seeking something, not necessarily the concrete tunnel or path to change, prior to its accidental or intentional discovery and that the act of seeking with a purpose created the condition of possibility for finding the way forward. When the close examination of personal limits reveals their permeability, in a similar vein, the implication is that effort was put forth into examining personal limits for some prior motivating reason or purpose in the first place, further implying a preexisting intentionality within imagination toward the answer.

However, there will be times when one stumbles across profundity, when one accidentally discovers either the permeability of limits or the hidden tunnel to a new way of being. This does not mean, however, that one possesses the ability to recognize them immediately as such. Intentionality to some degree must be involved or any discovered "profound" intentional object within the familiar will blend in with other "less profound" objects and will themselves appear less radiant than their worth. The ability to recognize the rarity of these discoveries depends on a person's openness to possibility, which is itself a function of the familiar. The inverse relationship between openness and familiarity means that as openness increases, familiarity decreases, and that as openness decreases, familiarity increases. Tunnels and permeability exist, by definition, outside the perceptual awareness of the one bound to the familiar. People are less open to discovering novelty to the degree that they find comfort in average everydayness, in the repetitive and habitual, in the common, in the rote and routine, and in the familiar.

Imagining that limits have permeability in fact makes limits permeable. Recognizing that our perception of limits is in itself limited and incomplete paves the way to transcend them. Looking with purpose and desire for something different makes finding different things possible. But to the degree that one does not seek, one also does not find. And to the degree that one does not ask, one also does not receive. And one's lack of faith in their own quest colors whatever is found or missed while on that quest. Change "might have been there all along" in the tunnel or in the permeable; however, both went unnoticed without an effort to the contrary. Therefore we can say that change occurs through the unification of *action*—desiring, seeking, asking, knocking, *imagination*—believing, having faith, and envisioning the future possible beyond habitual limitation, and *purpose*—the object of desire, the telos of determination, and the final causality of seeking, asking, and knocking, the "that" for the sake of which, *within imagination*, that pulls and stretches one forward into the new, *and is made concrete with choice*. Action, imagination, purpose, and choice co-emerge and each is meaningful, in a reverent kind of way, when considered in isolation or as a gestalt.

Let us return our gaze to the table of our couple where man and woman stare transfixed on the other in the most rudimentary stage of action, imagination, purpose and choice. In his advance toward her and in her body language toward him, each has already announced their intention, that is, each projects themselves forward into a primordial future with the other. In the short time from when he noticed her, and she him, and throughout his approach to her, and her response to him, the spark of creation birthed a new universe between them, each filled with imaginations about the other and anticipations of what could be with the other. Both know nothing about the other, anticipation being the loudest hatchling in the nest, yet the space separating them gradually shrinks with each step, transforming public space into social space, social space into personal space, and personal space into shared intimate space. As space changes, interacting with others becomes less possible, but interacting with the mark becomes more possible. What smoldered in public burns hotter in private, with lesser space adding more fuel to flame, the pursuit of knowledge and truth retreat to the background, allowing carnal desire to charge into the foreground. "What is" between them is indebted to their "not yet" together, their unrealized future more real to them than the trivialities of conversation such as speaking, laughing, drinking, and touching. These are but a means to an end.

He knows nothing about her existing relationships, about her legion of "friends," or about the wreckage from failed relationships strewn across her shore. He sees her not as she is, but as he wants her to be, and as she shows herself to be within this particular moment. He does not suspect that she is a replicant or that she harbors, at once, designs for him and secrets from him beyond the obvious, beyond his eye's adjustment to its predestined placement along the electromagnetic spectrum. He cannot see her as she is because evolution designed him not to see her in such a manner—she is for mating not for understanding. Nor does he desire to see her as she is, at least, not yet—not until he feels threatened by the relationship's death. For now, he interprets her at face value, according to his ability, knowing no other way, through the blemishes in his lens, through the limits of his own consciousness, and what she means to him at this moment is as much a function of his desire for her as it is her willingness to fulfill it. It is not the time to discuss nuance, threads, tapestries, ghosts, or how each finds themselves and creates meaning for themselves in the familiar. For him, it is a time to rejoice! Her smile means the end of his dark night. But as observers, we know that all dark nights begin with a smile.

As a woman's mystery and power depend upon her deception and secrecy, an inauthentic intentionality whose purpose it is to gather a crowd of potential suitors from which to soak attention and validation, all at once or each individually. A man's vulnerability also depends upon deceit, on his self-deception in the face of her deception; he is weak to the degree that he accepts her at face value. His power resides within his confidence to withstand deceit from himself to himself, from others to himself, and from himself to others. To the extent that men fool themselves about women's motivations, they are vulnerable to them. For fallen women, sex and intimacy are nothing more than tools, as both serve as a means to an end meant to dull the wits of men and bend them and mold them to her whim and purpose. He sacrifices his will to power to the extent that he submits to her pleasure. Her task is to addict him to her sweet, irresistible, and narcotic siren's flesh through sight and song, seduction and lust, and fantasy and feigned submission, to use every technique evolution provides at her disposal, to change him from the man who attracted her in the first place to the man she wants him to be, a toothless and obedient tiger, an indebted servant who exchanges his freedom and power, who surrenders his resources for her mind-numbing hugs, kisses, and affection. Women accept the currency of attention and validation from all who fall at their feet and use physical intimacy, or the promise of it, to hold close all those in her orbit from inside the boundaries of the friendship cage.

To the degree that a man allows his biological imperative to take him prisoner, to the degree that he clings to the flesh, his limits strengthen and familiarity's grip tightens. Although in his frustration and loneliness, he is most open to new possibilities, it is difficult for him to see new possibilities when blinded by old evolution. When he bends his knee to instinct, his intellect lowers, and he becomes susceptible to evolution's harbinger, and without the prior wherewithal to bind himself to his ship's mast, he will jump into the sea and he will surely die. For the slim chance to fulfill his main biological drive, he is willing to exchange his life without hesitation, for example, place himself in harm's way to rescue the damsel in distress, "white knight" for her when he sees her under threat, and support her and her bad choices, blindly, when she sheds tears with helpless whimpers, the arrows of women. Indeed, he is eager to spill his blood on her behalf and to suffer so that she does not have to, enabling her to escape unharmed into the arms of the man she really wants. Instead of rewarding he who sacrificed with hugs, kisses, and intimacy, as is his fantasy, she will acknowledge his pain with a simple "thanks" and will remind him that his blood and pain do not entitle him to her pleasure. She feels no obligation to reciprocate the man's sacrifice. Without blinking, he offers himself up in order for another man to bed her. Observers, it is better to walk away and leave women to deal with the consequences of their choices alone—do not involve yourselves!

Even though evolution has endowed both males and females with strategies to propagate the species, their method of accomplishing evolution's design differ. One method relies on secrets and plausible deniability, i.e., women want men to believe that they are having less sex less often with less men, the other method relies on transparent power and the public demonstration of virility, i.e., men want women to believe that they are having more sex more often with more women. Women desire potent men because the frequency of his bedroom successes reflect his social desirability and few things delight a woman more than when she dethrones another woman. She gloats to her competitor, "Even though you have him, he still wanted me." It is no secret that human males desire regular sex, companionship, and eventually children.[55] It is also no secret that the majority of men do not allow a woman's status to influence his decision to bed her, whereas a woman will for a man. For example, a man of high status, such as a wealthy doctor or a lawyer, will bed a woman of lower status, such as a school teacher or his long-distance friend. Neither match the man's resources or education level, a fact that the doctor or lawyer knows before moving forward with her.

From a masculine perspective through an evolutionary lens, youth, beauty, and fertility are a woman's greatest resource regardless of her career choice. Most men would not allow a woman's low-status to interfere with his lust, provided that she possessed youth, beauty, and fertility. These low-status women might not even care that their high-status counterpart already has a partner, as women have no problem sharing a man they perceive as having a higher sexual marketplace value than themselves, at least at first. A higher status woman, on the other hand, such as a supermodel or a wealthy heiress, will not lower her mate selection requirements and will not grant mating access to a common waiter or to someone whom she perceives as having a lower sexual market value than herself. Sometimes, higher status women will pair off with a lower status man either as a consequence of frustration or in order to maintain security and control. She often settles with a lower status man because she could not capture a man with a higher status than herself and chooses "the best among the worst." All men belonging to this order are always her second choice—her backup plan.

Knowledge of male motivation is so common that both mothers and fathers will often warn their young daughters about the carnal intentions of males in general and will attempt to impart their wisdom and

---

55   Coach Red Pill. (2019, February 8). *You can get only three things from a woman* [Video]. YouTube. https://www.youtube.com/watch?v=MLgxd2EYnmI

knowledge to her through anecdotes and stories designed to empower her to withstand the onslaught of male lust. Human females learn, sooner rather than later, to decipher male motivation and intention lest they mate with an impotent or deceitful man unable to provide for their needs and the needs of their children. Men learn about the world; women learn about men. Human males usually want to bed as many women as possible in order to impregnate as many as possible, "to spread their seed far and wide," and they usually do not keep their conquests secret unless there's a very good reason to do so, for example, his partner is in a committed relationship already and he does not mind being the "side dude." Men often brag to one another, share stories, and describe how this woman is better in bed than that woman in an attempt to build social credit concerning their potency. Men are attracted to women's youth, health, and fertility as demonstrated through their physical beauty and have no interest in hiding this fact. Such is a man's prime directive, and he will spend his life pursuing wealth, resources, and social status to attract mates. "The better he is able to provide for himself," her reasoning goes, "the better able he will be to provide for me and my children."

A casual inspection of the insect and animal kingdom reveals similar male mating strategies employed by the simple creatures therein. Some species of male birds, for example, must first build a nest to the female's satisfaction in order to seduce her. Other species of birds require that the male dance while displaying colorful feathers as a means to attract a mate. Human males, in a similar vein, must acquire physical strength and power in order to hunt and accumulate food and resources, must learn to cooperate with other members of the tribe in a division of labor while at the same time competing against other members for better mating opportunities, and do all that he can in order to improve himself to make himself more attractive to the feminine gaze. Males, whether insect, animal, or human, often fight one another, sometimes to the death, in order to keep dominant status or overthrow the current dominant to have access to the harem of females who stand at the ready to receive the victor. With humans, the male's confidence in himself, in his ability to acquire and provide resources, in his skill to coordinate and lead the hunt or farm the land, in his intellectual abilities to decipher all manner of obstacles, in his ability to manifest the strength of his character through his flesh catches the attention of human females. Such men demonstrate potency and high sexual marketplace value through their accomplishments. All that a man does to improve himself must be out in the open for communal evaluation, lest he go unnoticed by females and be deemed impotent by them. Men combat one another, fight their own laziness, rail against intellectual and physical limits in an effort to become self-sustaining leaders; women, on the other hand, wait at the finish line and bed the winners. Women are the gatekeepers of sex and control the propagation of the species through mate selection.[56] It is a man's evolutionary purpose to make himself worthy of being selected. All the efforts of a man are realized in the moment when a woman accepts him or denies him access to mating benefits.

Not all men possess the determination or the strength of will to fight themselves and stand firm in their code and in their values.[57] Not all men know how to navigate loneliness, solitude, social rejection, and imposed isolation. Some men are simpler than others, weaker than others, and never stand apart from their peers. Rather than asserting strength and dominance, these men assert submission. And while they share the same biological mandate to acquire regular sex, comfort and companionship,

---

56   Russell D. C. & Hatfield, E. (1989). Gender differences in receptivity to sexual offers. *Journal of Psychology & Human Sexuality, 2:1, 39–55,* DOI: 10.1300/J056v02n01_04

57   Essential Truth. (2018, July 27). *Jordan Peterson: Men who make the worst partners* [Video]. YouTube. https://www.youtube.com/watch?v=bJor1Z2LG0Y

and children, nothing about them is extraordinary and they implement self-degrading alternative methods to acquire sex and resources. They are birds without a nest and without colorful feathers, birds who are content to perch all day long and never sing out, lest they disturb others. They do not inspire others to follow their leadership, they lack a clear vision of the future and the passion to obtain it, and they are generally unsure of themselves in matters great and small. Many find them awkward, inept, and tiresome. Others find them simple, boring, deficient, lacking, substandard, and undeserving. They cannot and do not motivate themselves or others to evolve; they produce leaves and branches, but no fruit.[58] You might find them reading self-improvement books, but never putting the words into action. They are always anxious and unsure. They do not seek deep understanding, they do not command their own emotions, they do not ask for wisdom, and they do not risk knocking on doors, lest they disturb others with the sound of knuckle meeting wood. They would rather accept lies than the truth and passively accept their place in the universe as a matter of unchangeable fact. These men do not take risks or put themselves in harm's way in order to "play it safe."[59] They do not open themselves to opportunities and they shirk away from responsibility and hard work. These men have little to no experience with women except the experience gained from worshipping them, putting them on a pedestal, and making every effort to ensure their comfort. They are essentially a hard penis sitting on a couch in solitude; one should not be surprised at their attitude because even bacteria breed. They draw sustenance from feasting upon another man's leftovers, are happy being the second choice, and will look the other way if he suspects infidelity because having someone is better than having no one at all. These men

---

58 Mt. 21:19

59 Mt. 25:25-26

are known as "simps" because they value submission not self-domination, passivity not activity, the status quo not making waves, blending in not standing apart, and mediocrity not seeking or asking for anything beyond their own self-imposed limits.

Their intent is not to pursue the object of their desire but to sit idly by with a patient and yearning hope that the object of their desire will come to them. They believe that if they are nice enough for long enough, women will eventually see and appreciate their sweet and harmless disposition and grant mating benefits. Women abhor such men. Women do not respect such men. But women's genuine disdain for them does not invalidate their usefulness to her. From the simp's point of view, his patience eventually pays off and from her point of view, she will always have a reliable backup plan. The simp will be her beta male provider after she is finally ready to "settle down," having been run through and turned out by legions of alphas. Betas pay for what alphas got for free, whether that payment be in terms of dinner and dates, various tokens of affection, parenting, conversational energy, or the rehabilitation of her spirit; she imposes rules, limits, and various conditions upon betas, while never having imposed those same rules upon alphas. Consistency, it would seem, depends upon the particular male, the degree to which she fancies him, and the perceived benefit he provides to her.

She knows about beta males and picks them second for a reason.[60] They are easier to control and manipulate and pose little to no threat to her habitual comfort. She knows that she will always be the alpha's second choice, and therefore chooses a beta to be her second choice so that she might shine forth as the beta's first choice. When she feeds her simp acolyte regular scraps of sex from her table, knowing she will never

---

60   BlackRam313. (2020, January 19). *Beta male game: What it is and why it works.* [Video]. YouTube. https://www.youtube.com/watch?v=RTzXGl0vhiM

give the same food portions to him that she gave to the alphas, what little of his mind numbs. With little protest, he surrenders any ambition to influence and inspire her to become a better human being. She uses pleasures of the flesh to quell emotional rebellion, to distract from trials and tribulations, and to side-step glaring contradictions. In short, she provides the beta with sex in order to safeguard her secrets. Drug addicts crave drugs and alcoholics crave alcohol; simps crave sexual pleasure and the attention, validation, and sedation that sexual acceptance represents. Loving a simp means that she chooses to be with someone who will never inspire her to be a better person, which as a calculated decision, removes more troublesome personal responsibility from her plate. She disarms and extinguishes the beta's arguments, disagreements, and conflicts with all manners of sex and takes resentful comfort knowing that she has a reliable, stable, and tolerant acolyte. Part of her loves her beta, part of her hates him. She cherishes the stability and reliability he provides and resents him for his dimwittedness that allows her to walk all over him with impunity.

She adopts the masculine energy he surrenders. A woman who feels the need to dominate and be in control, a stereotypically masculine trait, will eventually seek out and find feminine men upon whom to exercise her authority after her pursuit of strong, high-value men ends in disappointment or failure. She will have a history of failed past relationships where her male partner was dominate, perhaps too dominating, and as a consequence, her disdain for them leads her to find submissive men more interesting or at least less threatening, and she will say with plausible deniability that, given her past, she "needs" and "likes" a man with a softer disposition. The reality is that she will never abandon strong men from her past; rather, she will keep them in her orbit as "platonic friends," allowing her to feed upon her imagination of them while planted in mediocre stability. In this manner, she enjoys the pleasures of both worlds simultaneously for one is never enough.

A beta man provides her with affection, attention, cash and prizes, children, comfort, conversation, distraction, drinks, entertainment, food, intimacy, lethargy, orgasm, reliability, stability, and validation—precisely the things that she never required alphas to provide beforehand in order to ensure mating access. Her beta "loves her," will "always be there for her," and would not mind remaining "friends" should their relationship together fail, even if the failure rested upon her shoulders for covert infidelity with other men.

The one thing a beta man can never provide to her is inspiration. He will never stir her to be a better human being, just a cleverer one. She takes pride in knowing how his simple mind works and uses this knowledge to better hide her secrets in plain sight. She will never fully emotionally surrender herself to him; she cannot imagine opening the chaos of her mind and heart to a man whom she knows will be over-powered by the darkness inside her. His default answer is "I don't know." She trusts in neither his abilities nor his strength. But in his defense, his appeal to her never depended upon his strength of intellect or body in the first place. Strong and able men are harder to control, you see, and this is why she preys upon the weak. Because of her beta's ineptitude, she keeps her legion of male friends close and relies upon them, in a thousand little ways, to provide her with what her beta cannot: stimulating conversations, fantasies about surrendering control, and wealth, resources, and strong masculine attention. Women who choose beta males are the ones who rob the fruit grown in one relationship to feed a man in another, purport monogamy yet experience either emotional or physical polygamy themselves in secret with others, and deploy replicants to enjoy the benefits of multiple relationships on multiple levels with multiple people simultaneously.

Weak men implement alternative strategies meant to accomplish evolution's purpose. He never bothers looking for patterns in her behavior, emotions, or thought processes. He remains gullible and accepts her words and explanations for the sake of "trust" at face value. He wants to believe, so desperately, that she loves him as much as he loves her. Nothing could be further from the truth. As a rule, women do not love men the same way that men love women. He may suspect that she has other men on the side, but will never object to her "friendships" in order to protect his access to constant sexual benefits. He is happy to be used, happy to be the second choice, and happy to embrace someone instead of loneliness. He is the puppet and she the puppet master. She is the brain, and he is the brawn. She decides his emotional diet and dictates the terms of his happiness to him and he accepts. He is compliant, complacent, and soft. He submits to her will for love's sake, and she resents him for it.

Weak men have their origin as well. All male children, strong and weak alike, arrived here much in the same way the woman did, with the differences between them growing more obvious as they age. In the uterus, males and females resemble one another during the first eighteen to twenty weeks of pregnancy, as is common knowledge in the medical community, and in their infancy, each experiences the same hunger pain that instinctually forced them to cry out to the world. The brain's need for nutrients rendered the placenta and umbilical cord insufficient, as growing brains require more sugar and fat from breastmilk to sustain their rapid physiological formation. Outside the womb, what their brain cannot use immediately, their bodies store as reserve, and this is why we adults take delight in seeing plump little babies. Adults know, with all other things being equal, that fat babies stand a better chance of survival and are healthier than skinny babies.

After birth, each begins to trust or mistrust along similar lines, influenced by either seeing welcoming faces or not, by either experiencing the bliss of pain's removal or not, and neither infant knows who or what they are or to which gender they belong. All they know is pain or comfort, warmth or cold, and light or dark. This phase of their development is not meant to actualize higher order thinking, but rather, to lay the physiological foundations for that kind of thinking. The primordial relationship between parent and child also begins to take shape and it lays the groundwork through which other future relationships will appear.

It is clear, even minutes after their birth, that infants possess the ability to imitate their adult caregivers. After the baby's physical needs have been met, positioning the baby's face twelve inches away from the adult's face, as the infant has yet to master fine motor control over the ocular muscles, reveals an interesting phenomenon when the adult sticks their tongue out and in for the infant to see. This is an example of nonverbal teaching, the first proof of the concrete endowment from a preexisting sociality to a newborn's individuality. After a few moments of visible confusion, the infant will focus their attention on the adult's tongue, seeing it go in and out of their mouth, and will mimic the effort themselves. Upon witnessing the success of the experiment, the adult will display smiles and visual and audible excitement, which the infant imitates as well. In the crudest sense, the baby learns that its tongue movement elicits a response from adults.

If an infant is able to imitate an adult's tongue movement minutes after birth, how much more, less obvious information, is the baby taking in to imitate? What kind of emotional energy saturates its environment, how often do adults bathe it in love and care, and how many adults deliberately and consistently model the behaviors that they want the child to adopt one day? With an infant's tongue, all adults owe their interpretation and implementation of their independence to their social referential framework given from youth, the first, deepest, and best hidden blemish in their lens, the first thread woven into the first tapestry, the first nuance from mother and father, the first foreground, the first background, the first hunger, and the first trust or mistrust.

Eventually the infant turns into a child, the child turns into an adolescent, and the adolescent turns into an adult. Man and woman combine together, each surrounded by the ghosts of who others are to them and who they are to others, fractions of their relational heart divided among the legion of people involved with their life. Observers should never underestimate the intoxicating power of the honeymoon phase. New lovers will use all manner of intellect, emotion, and behavior to fortify their position with each other in order to keep the rest of the world out so that they are left alone to delight themselves in the other, with the other, through the other, and because of the other. They will speak of how much they "love" the other; outsiders could not possibly even begin to comprehend the uniqueness of the "love" toward the other. "No one in the history of love has loved like us," they will say. Frequent copulations and messy orgasms reinforce their codependence as each now requires the other to create and sustain personal meaning. Journeying alongside the other toward a mutual goal is one thing; abdicating personal responsibility or defining personal freedom and responsibility in terms of the other, depending upon them and them alone for personal happiness and meaning is another. This is the definition of inauthenticity. The other, absent in the hours, days, weeks, months, or years prior to the first consummation, is now interpreted as a necessary component to achieve and maintain personal happiness.

In this moment they now share together, no one dares challenge them otherwise with information potentially undermining their intoxicated happiness, lest the lovers unite to defend their illusory castle built upon metaphorical sand. "Why is our relationship any of your business?" they ask. "How can I ignore someone drowning, especially when I know them, have interacted with them, and know what must be done to save their lives?" the outsider replies. "We are not drowning. Leave us alone." Even though an outsider's perspective on the lover's relationship might reveal their individual shortcomings and offer a pathway toward improvement, wise counsel always falls on deaf ears to those who "love" without "understanding." They interpret the outsider's genuine concern as a clear and present danger to the kingdom they built together and for every concern the outsider raises, each partner responds with dozens of arrows evidencing the contrary.

All of this would be fine and good except that experience shows that sometimes love ends between those who were, once upon a time, the most confident and prideful in their love. What once grew together now grows apart; friends who loved together, are now strangers living apart. That which was once so fiercely defended is now dust and ash underfoot. The outsider's prophecy came to pass; the lovers ignored his message in order to preserve the elation from neurochemical intoxication and mutual sexual stimulation. For them, love was nothing more than a momentary orgasm supported with "feelings" and actions designed to bring about the next copulation. This is why immature love always expresses itself as leaping from one sexual encounter to another. This kind of love requires constant assurance to keep it real and each feels compelled to bind themselves to the other's presence. Even when apart, frequent text messages, numerous pictures, and countless phone conversation act as a conduit and as a symptom for their unhealthy attachment; without frequent sex, the "love" between them dies. Rather than sex and intimacy being chosen as one expression from among the many other expressions of love, it is the sole expression, the lowest common denominator designed to achieve evolution's goal. How could such a love fail? Love that depends on the flesh and the flesh alone always fails. A love that seeks itself from itself, that compounds upon itself in order to satisfy itself never grows beyond itself; this kind of love mistakes its own "vibration" as movement and believes that its circular merry-go-round spinning means growth, transformation, and discovery. But it does not. When love's intentional object is another human being, love cannot grow beyond the other's limits because it requires the other's limits to manifest itself. This "love" is content in the familiar within the boundaries of the other's manifestation. After a while, novelty gives way to routine and all the sex in the world cannot mend what was broken from the start.

Dear observer, let us synthesize our discussion thus far and alter our perceptual lens in light of the concepts described. Evolution concerns itself with the propagation of the species, not with the protection of feelings. It is in the interest of both men and women to create the strongest children, physically, mentally, and emotionally, and selecting a strong, intelligent, youthful, fertile, and beautiful mate for copulation increases the likelihood of producing high-quality offspring. Over thousands of years, both males and females evolved mating strategies to filter defective contenders in order to set the stage to create the strongest, smartest, and most well-rounded human being possible. Some men have developed a proactive mating strategy, other men have adopted a reactive mating strategy.

Unlike animals and insects, human beings are aware of evolution's influence on motivation and purpose, and while this awareness does not alter the drive to reproduce, it does make for interesting alternatives to accomplish its mandate. Human beings can choose to mate with this person or that person, irrespective of their sexual marketplace value, accomplishing the drive to multiply without fulfilling the need to be fruitful beforehand,[61] i.e., to many, the commandment to "be fruitful and multiply" equivocates with "multiply then be fruitful." The former requires one to be fruitful first, that is, to implement a conscious effort to increase personal value through study and exercise. The latter, on the other hand, translates to mating privileges granted irrespective of value and effort. Because males and females achieve sexual maturity during adolescence, well before establishing intellectual, emotional, and spiritual maturity, chaos and disorder sometimes ensues between them, leading to unnecessary pain, hurt, suffering, misunderstanding, and confusion. Emphasizing physical pleasure lessens emotional collateral damage.

Women attract with secrets while men attract with prowess. Some men even attract with submission. A woman keeps legions of suitor-friends close to her heart in secret while a man showcases his wealth, power, social status, and other endowments for women to behold in public. Man and woman affix their gaze on one another, playing the other's game, using all manner of techniques and tactics from evolution either to seduce or be seduced by the other, each a pawn positioned on the other's chessboard for bedroom checkmate. Each strategizes plans within plans for the other, moves and countermoves, contingencies stacked upon contingencies, and each possesses a treasure trove of reasons and justifications with

---

61   Gn. 1:28

ample evidence, both pros and cons, to convince themselves and others of in-the-moment thoughts, feelings, and behaviors.

So much for multiplying. In the proper way of understanding, "being fruitful" both precedes and is a necessary condition for "multiplying." Truth, love, wisdom, and clarity as intentional objects must precede the act of seeking, asking, and knocking that brings them about, meaning both that one experiences a certain yearning for them from within their own ignorance of them and that one desires them through their own unclear perception of them. Within the boundaries of limitation, one imagines transcending limitation; the act of imagining transcendence is precisely what makes achieving it possible. People change because they want it to be so, even if that change defies the instinct to seek pleasure and avoid pain, forsaking the flesh for righteousness sake. The act of choosing manifests desire, making stretching beyond it possible, and paves the way for grasping the fruit that was once upon a time out of reach.

Being fruitful means bearing fruit, and knowing a person means knowing their fruit.[62] Stated in another manner, we can make safe assumptions about a person from the consequences or results that manifest in their wake. Observers enact this principle in their study of "breadcrumbs" or "data points," and observers push the point further with "deductions about tapestries from threads" and "deductions about threads from tapestries." In both the New Testament and Old Testament, what we observers label "data points" or "breadcrumbs" are called "fruit," and our observational principles remain consistent regardless of the nomenclature: we make "deductions about the tree from its fruit," and we make "deductions about the fruit from its tree."

---

62   Mt. 7:16

The production of fruit is the result of much effort. As the farmer of his own life, each man must determine and decide the best soil to plant his seeds. Prior to making this critical beginning determination, he must inform himself through careful observation where the other fruit trees enjoy the greatest success. He observes the quality of the soil that produces the healthiest trees, and plants his seed there or in similar soil elsewhere. Unwise farmers plant their seed without considering the soil, the amount of sunlight, access to water, or his own ability to nurture seeds, saplings, and trees. The unwise farmer does not take into account the predators who would dig up and feast upon his labor, the elements that would wash away his effort, or the kind of fertilizer needed to produce the healthiest crop.

Dear observer, I implore you to heed the words of the one who taught me:

"A sower went out to sow his seed. Now as he sowed, some fell on the edge of the path and was trampled on; and the birds of the air ate it up. Some seed fell on a rock, and when it came up it withered away, having no moisture. Some seed fell in the middle of thorns and the thorns grew with it and choked it. And some seed fell into good soil and grew and produced its crop a hundredfold. Saying this the sower cried, 'Anyone who has ears for listening should listen!'"

His disciples asked him what this parable might mean, and he said, "To you is granted to understand the secrets of the kingdom of God; for the rest it remains in parables so that they may look but not perceive, listen but not understand."[63]

"This, then, is what the parable means: the seed is the word of God. Those on the edge of the path are people who have heard it, and then

---

63   Is. 6:9

the devil comes and carries away the word from their hearts in case they should believe and be saved. Those on the rock are people who, when they first hear it, welcome the word with joy. But these have no root; they believe for a while, and in time of trial, they give up. As for the part that fell into thorns, this is people who have heard, but as they go on their way, they are choked by the worries and riches and pleasures of life and never produce any crops. As for the part in the rich soil, this is people with a noble and generous heart who have heard the word and take it to themselves and yield a harvest through their perseverance."[64]

---

64 Lk. 8:1-15

CHAPTER FOUR

> **"**
> *Because the accuracy of these instruments depends on the teacher's and the student's clarity during their use, their task will be to identify structures in their consciousness that either impede or enable clarity.*

FRACTIONS OF LONELINESS

In order to move forward with you in our discussion together, I must lay my mind naked before you.[65] Through my descriptions presented across various observations thus far, you have begun to comprehend certain fractions of my soul, threads within my tapestry, nuances concerning certain topics, fruits of my tree, and breadcrumbs and data points about this matter or that matter. As we move along together, you should further develop and sharpen the skill necessary to reverse-engineer my discussions in order to reveal "me" as the one doing the discussing. The more

---

65   Gn. 3:7

we interact and the more varied our interactions are together, the more different sides of me "come into the light," so to speak, for you to sum to achieve an understanding, should you seek it. I am no different than the people we observe and you should implement the same techniques to understand me as you do to understand those whom we observe together; I do not possess some magical transcendental ego floating above it all observing thoughts, feelings, and behaviors from others in their purity. I, too, am the perceptual lens that focuses objects of consciousness into the foreground and background of my mind. I also perceive the world with my biases, through my biases, and because of my biases like everyone else. There are those whom I love and those who dig into my heart with disappointment and frustration. I have witnessed new life being born and have said goodbye to friends and family now sleeping in the grave. My spirit is battle-worn and there are times I grow sick with experience.

But such is life to those who travel from one horizon to the next, seeking truth and expanding knowledge and wisdom gained along the way from this experience or that—the result of my different relationships with different people at different times in my own life. Sometimes, I was the master and they were the student. Other times, I was the student and they were the master. Looking back on what was, I learned much about myself from the students when I was the master, and my ego humbled when I was the student apprenticing under someone stronger and smarter than myself. True masters are eternal students themselves, always seeking—students who finally learned how to learn and desire to pass on their wisdom to the next generation in order to save them from expending time in trial and error.

What should be so simple is not. Man should love woman and woman should love man. Individually, each should strive toward greater wisdom, truth, knowledge, and insight, and on their solo travel toward something greater than themselves, each should encounter the other, then and only then, and choose to walk together toward the same destination. But this is not the case. Man discovers woman or woman discovers man and halts in awe of the other, making the other the object of worship, no longer concerned about seeking or asking for greater things. Instead of continuing the ascension together, they stop and intertwine themselves together, mistaking delights of the flesh for delights of the spirit. For many, mud offers a solace that the breath of life cannot.

I have spent much of my life pursuing the understanding of the relationship between man and woman, between Adam and Eve. I believe that all men descended from Adam inherited his strengths and weaknesses, and that all women share in Eve's virtues and vices. The unification of Adam and Eve's flesh created children whose spirit received greater or lesser concentrations of each parent's tainted spiritual essence. Eve's virtues and vices will therefore be present, to more or less degree, in all of Adam's descendants. Similarly, Eve's descendants, whether male or female, will embody their father's strengths and weaknesses. This concept of "spiritual inheritance" exemplifies as humanity's physical inheritance of the first breath. God breathed His own breath of life into Adam's nostrils,[66] animating the mud, and Eve inherited the breath Adam received from God at her creation without God delivering a second breath. Eve's children breathe as their mother and father did, and every descendent from them continues to breathe to this day—what God first put into motion with Adam repeats to this day. All of us breathe today because Adam breathed so long ago.

66 Gn. 2:7

The concept of spiritual inheritance is nothing new. The early Christians recognized that everyone inherited Adam's corrupted spiritual essence as sin: "Well then; it was through one man that sin came into the world, and through sin death, and thus death has spread through the whole human race because everyone has sinned."[67] "No distinction is made: all have sinned and lack God's glory."[68] Additionally, the author of the Book of Psalms in the Old Testament also recognized Adam's foundational transgression: "Yahweh looks down from heaven at the children of Adam. To see if a single one is wise, a single one seeks God. All have turned away, all alike turned sour, not one of them does right, not a single one."[69] However, spiritual inheritance is not limited to sin alone, though all else perceived "beyond sin" occurs "after sin" and must pass "through sin," our fallen lens, in order to appear within our fallen consciousness. All human beings perceive through sin, with sin, and because of sin. Unescapable proof of this can be found among the dead in the cemetery.[70]

Humanity has also inherited a remembrance of Eden, the time before the fall, when God walked with us[71] and angels, as disembodied intellect, conversed with us, studied us, and all created things dwelled with us. Although imperfectly remembered through the veil of sin, memories of Eden decorate the interior landscape of all who feel abandoned, alienated, betrayed, contemplative, curious, disappointed, excited, glorious, happy, harmonious, inquisitive, joyful, lonely, luminous, peaceful, and sorrowful and all other emotions far and wide. Everything between man

---

67   Rom: 5:12

68   Rom. 3:23

69   Ps. 14:2-3

70   Rom. 6:23

71   Gn. 3:8

and woman, whether positive or negative, first appeared in Eden between Adam and Eve, and to their descendants were passed the first thoughts, emotions, behaviors, and memories.

Adam's loneliness, in particular, caught my attention. Everyone from Eve onward inherited this loneliness similar to how we all inherited the first breath. In Genesis 2:18, God observes that "It is not right that the man should be alone." He made this observation prior to the fall and prior to the creation of Eve, meaning that Adam's loneliness was pure, without evil, and that it was something woven into the human soul by God. I imagine Adam and God conversing about its meaning and purpose after its discovery, as everything else in creation followed God's design; created beings perceive the purpose of some things immediately and other things gradually. God could have easily created Adam without this loneliness to be sure, but did not, because it was His design that it be filled by Eve later on. This is why, dear observer, men desire women. It is not that we crave women for pleasures of the flesh alone, but that we need a woman to cast out the loneliness within.

Even though Adam had no referential frame to understand and process loneliness, he felt it and God perceived the motion in Adam's heart. Perhaps Adam felt something lacking after interacting with the various angels, each of them having a unique disposition according to their desire and ability. Perhaps Adam saw that angels had others of their kind, masculine and feminine energies spread among them, and perceived the pleasure each had while interacting with others. He could not find in himself what he saw in others.

Adam and the angels conversed, and through their various conversations together, Adam learned something from them about how each drew a unique pleasure interacting with others of their kind whose pleasure was obedient to, yet different from, those pleasures bestowed directly from God. Sociality within another like himself was an experience that he desired in the quiet of his heart, an experience similar to his angelic brethren, but in his unique way. While the Genesis account makes no reference to Adam bringing his concern directly to God, I imagine that Adam and God shared an openness covering all topics great and small. Genesis tells us that God perceived Adam's loneliness, anticipating his need before the need vocalized or was prayed about, and created the wild animals and birds of the heavens as a means of making a helper for him to end the loneliness.[72]

Of course, God knew beforehand that Adam would not select an animal, bird, or angel as a helper to end his loneliness, and therefore, the process of creating animals and birds was meant for some other reason. God already knew what Adam came to realize for himself: the creation of things precisely *not* his helper frustrated him in some fashion, amplifying both his loneliness and his desire to end it, which made sweeter the presentation of Eve. "This one at last is bone of my bones and flesh of my flesh!" Adam exclaimed.[73] Eve was Adam's "at last." He was finally able to present himself to another of his kind. He could have chosen to remain alone, but did not. He could have chosen an angel as his helper, but did not. Eve, for Adam, was his answer. Finally, he was able to receive spiritual and mental stimulation from someone who was similar yet different than himself. He had someone to take care of him and comfort him in a manner that neither God nor angel could; the flesh taken from Adam is the flesh that he chooses to comfort him. His loneliness terminated and he found a new purpose in creation: to bond with his mate and to offer

---

72   Gn. 2:18-19

73   Gn. 2:23

to her all the fruits of his intellect and spirit. Making her smile gave him a deeper purpose, and the pure relationship between them reflected the order and love that the creator bestowed upon His creation. God wanted Adam to be comforted and designed Eve for him and Adam for her, that each may be pleased with the other by the hand of the creator.

One can imagine that some length of time passed after Eve's creation, before the fall, when Adam and Eve discovered one another in both flesh and spirit. Their relationship grew. She was similar to him, but different, as the angels, animals, and trees differ from one another yet they are still similar in at least sharing the same creator. Eve allowed Adam to discover aspects of himself unknown to himself until her creation. Eve also gradually grew to understand herself, her mate, her environment, and her God. Each apprehended with clarity in their own way, two souls similar yet distinct, expressing different flavors of emotion, thought, and behavior, inspiring more curiosity and discussion among their angelic brothers and sisters. Lucifer was one among them, observing from afar, as God denied him permission to interject himself directly into them. Lucifer used his keen and powerful intellect to deduce the weaknesses of each through distant observation. He did not need to be privy to their thoughts as he overheard their conversations, studied their body language, and advanced theories about their anticipated actions with one another. Over time, his deductions and mental experiments proved correct more often than incorrect, and when incorrect, he refined his craft, and he came to understand truths woven into the human heart for both the man and woman. Adam's weakness was Eve, he perceived, and Eve's weakness was herself. By appealing to her, he would capture them both, and taint the jewel of his Father's effort with himself. He knew that he could not force himself upon them, as the creator declared that no being was allowed to enter into them against free will, and therefore decided that he would use free will itself to have them open the door to their heart and mind to him.

Eve provided something to Adam that God either would not or did not; Adam found his fulfillment in her, filling the space God made for her within his heart, but Eve did not find duplicate fulfillment in her companion. She did love Adam but not in the way that Adam loved her. God did not imbue a unique loneliness into her, but instead relied on the structure of the loneliness taken from Adam's rib which was later individuated according to her spirit at her creation. To be clear, Adam's loneliness was a part of Eve, but her unique spirit shifted the original loneliness into something similar yet different within her. She knew that Adam was made for her and that she was made for him, but never fully surrendered herself to either him or God. Perhaps over time, Eve would have gradually opened herself up fully to her husband and to her God. She, like Adam, was well aware of God's mandate never to eat fruit from the tree of good and evil but was either more defiant or curious about the reason why. Adam found it easier to fall in line with God's command, learning and imitating the hierarchical order among the angels, seeing the harmony between higher ranks and lower ranks, each knowing their place according to their nature, ability, and desire. Lucifer knew that directly tempting Adam would fail, and was just as excited as Adam was, but for a different reason, after Eve's debut.

Lucifer, the first observer, came to know Eve from the accumulation of his observations and deductions from afar. He noticed that she would often stare at her own reflection in a still pond for long periods of time and that she put effort into beautifying her appearance in order to make herself more pleasing to her husband. Seeing her take strange delight in her own reflection after she altered her appearance with some external object revealed to Lucifer that she took unusual pleasure in herself, that her emotions were tied to her looks, and that she studied her outward appearance more intensely than the man. She was already pretty but desired to be prettier. This little observation is all that a fallen archangel needed to begin deducing and speculating. Adam, on the other hand, studied his reflection to pick food from his teeth and remove crumbled leaves from his hair. To him, his reflection was practical and not meaningful. He drew no delight from his appearance like the woman did and was more interested in cultivating Eden.

Lucifer took note of her temperament, her responses to Adam's questions, her body language and its emotional and behavioral correlate, and inferred the meaning in her words unspoken. From a distance, Lucifer came to know both Adam and Eve, and calculated their potential responses to his temptation. Lucifer is not all-knowing or all-powerful, but his disembodied intellect does not confine him to the same limits that neurons and flesh confine us. He is ageless and wise and studies his prey long before he makes his first pounce. All temptation crafted is customized to the one receiving it, according to the unique weaknesses and understandings that the person has. He studies us even to this day, having overheard thousands of conversations from billions of individuals across the millennia. He has witnessed how each person acts and reacts under different stimuli, how wording nuances produce different outcomes, and how each person processes different experiences throughout their lives. He remembers everything. His knowledge of humanity has come about through repeated observation, through trial and error, and through his countless experiences with us. After collecting and remembering billions of data points from billions of people over tens of thousands of years, I imagine that he knows us even better than we know ourselves without needing to read our mind.

He knew that Eve took delight in herself, something that Adam did not do, and crafted a plan to exploit her holy narcissism. First, he would arouse the curiosity in her heart with misdirection for something she knew that she should not possess. "Did God really say you were not to eat from *any* of the trees in the garden?"[74] Lucifer did not name the specific tree even though he knew its name. He feigned ignorance to clear more room for Eve to respond and purposely opened the dialogue between them with him at an artificial disadvantage. Second, he would acknowledge her objections and cleverly challenge them, fanning the flames of doubt within her heart using himself as the example of one who had eaten of the fruit, encouraging her secret desires with his proof, and seduce her with exaggerated comfort to go against her better judgment. "No! You will not die! God knows in fact that the day you eat it your eyes will be opened and you will be like gods, knowing good from evil."[75] Third, he would endorse and support her selfish decision, helping her to push thoughts of Adam out of her mind in order to make room for her own fantasies of what life would be like after tasting the forbidden. "The woman saw that the tree was good to eat and pleasing to the eye, and that it was *enticing for the wisdom that it could give*. So, she took some of its fruit and ate it."[76]

The most interesting part I find here was not that she found the fruit enticing for the wisdom that it could give, but that she still managed to find it enticing even after considering what both Adam and God

---

74   Gn. 3:1

75   Gn. 3:4-5

76   Gn. 3:6

already provided to her. For her to desire the forbidden even after walking and talking with both her husband and God in the garden, even after surrendering her body in sexual union with Adam, even after understanding how much she meant to Adam and his loneliness, and even after her conversations with various heavenly hosts, it meant that, from her point of view, all those endeavors did not measure up to the object of her desire. In other words, Eve found more meaning and enticement in her own desires than in Adam's love for her, than in God's love for her, than in her friendships with angels. For Eve, submitting to a thing is what beautifies a thing; had she submitted to either God or Adam, they would have appeared more desirable to her than the fruit.

This is why, dear observer, that some women in our modern time conjure up a plethora of reasons justifying their relational submission to a man, who through his own effort, is not worthy of her attention; the man might be lacking a will-to-power, but her desire of him is what beautifies and elevates him. Understand that, from a woman's point of view, more important than a man's inherent value is her own perceived and interpreted value of him; her *perception* of him makes him more than what he is. It is not so much that women love men as it is that women love what they see, or rather, *want* to see in men.

With Eve now fallen, Lucifer turned his attention to Adam but moved not from his place in the garden. Eve turned her back to the serpent in order to search for her mate in giddy delight, to share with him the object of her enticement. Her eyes now opened with knowledge forbidden, the proud new father welcomed the first of God's gems to his company. With relaxed composure and a smile that grew bigger with each new step she took, Lucifer basked in the knowledge that Eve would use Adam's love for her to claim the other gem for himself.

Upon discovering Adam, she made her presence known in the usual way. Before she spoke, she looked at him and he looked different. When he raised his concentrated gaze from weaving a wreath of flowers that he made for her,[77] her change of looks startled him and he dropped his gift. No longer was she the Eve from his dreams, but he clung to her nonetheless. He knew that she would die and that his loneliness would return. Both he and Eve perceived the distance between them growing while in each other's arms. The chasm within grew with each passing moment.

New thoughts of her abandonment and the pain she would endure from her loneliness without him entered his mind. The thought of him asking God to fashion a second Eve did not occur to him; he wanted the one woman, the first woman, who captured his imagination and inspired him to become a better and fuller man. "Never would her like be again," he mused to himself. Mercy and forgiveness were foreign concepts in Eden as never before were they needed; Adam did not know this side of God, nor did he trust that God would preserve his mate. He loved not in the spirit of sharing but in the spirit of codependence. Adam wanted to hold on to his first love eternally, and with a confident fear, decided that he would go with her into the darkness so she would not have to brave it by herself. "I will die with her so she does not have to die alone." With teary eye, Adam ate the fruit willingly and added the final gem to Lucifer's collection.

"If they loved you so much, Father, never would they have listened to me at all" he mocked. "I take the handiwork of your breath from you and now imbue it with my own essence, so that these two now have two Fathers: you and me.[78] What you have endowed with clarity, I fur-

---

77   Milton, J. (2003). *Paradise lost.* (J. Leonard, Ed.; 1st ed.). Penguin Classics.

78   Jn. 8:44

ther sharpen with myself. Their descendants cannot pursue you without pursuing me, and the pain you bestowed upon me must be shared with them in their capacity to bear it. And I shall forever watch and learn from them and their heirs as a parent watches and learns from their children, and I shall pour into them my wisdom in their capacity to absorb it. They are mine, or rather, ours. Now you will feel my loss billions of times over at the moment of their death, unless, of course, all of this was a mistake and you want to wipe the slate of creation clean. Father, their desires exceed their devotion to you. Eve loved herself more than you. Adam loved Eve more than you. And both love me more than you."

God did not withdraw his presence but rather removed Adam and Eve from it. "Now that the man has become like one of us in knowing good from evil, he must not be allowed to reach out his hand and pick from the tree of life too, and eat and live forever! So Yahweh God expelled him from the Garden of Eden, to till the soil from which he had been taken. He banished the man, and in front of the garden of Eden he posted the great winged creatures and the fiery flashing sword, to guard the way to the tree of life."[79] And the rest, as they say, is history. To this day, Adam's loneliness and Eve's narcissism are found in the hearts of both men and women along with Lucifer's intertwined essence. God's breath, too, mingles in the hearts of men and women, but never pronounces itself with dominating grandiosity even though we differentiate between life and death by the presence or absence of breath.

We can say with a relative degree of certainty that humanity's desire for love sprouts from a fundamental loneliness laid at the foundation of the world, that man's yearning for woman finds its roots in Adam's yearning for Eve, and that women entertain multiple loves simultaneously: the

---

79   Gn. 3:22-24

love for her companion and the love for herself. And that no matter what she shares with one partner, she will always have secrets in her heart for someone else or something else. We also observe that the human spirit is one part divine and good and one part fallen and corrupted and that dreams of peace, love, and happiness after never having known them is our distant remembrance of Eden.

Why is it that I adopt a religious interpretation for the human condition? The answer is simple, at least, simple to me. The knowledge of human beings is vast but also limited. In other words, human knowledge and wisdom are finite endeavors. In theory, there will eventually come a time where one knows much and understands everything under the sun,[80] and at that point, there will be no mysteries left for they have all been discovered. It is theoretically possible, although not likely, for a person to read every book ever written, entertain every thought born from the minds of fellow human beings, and become proficient in all matters of both intellect and emotion. In other words, humanity can aspire to match Lucifer, the first observer. A person can likewise rule every kingdom on earth, possess all the material wealth therein, and bed every woman who walks. But no matter the deeds done or the knowledge obtained, human beings still die. Looking to a divine interpretation of humanity removes human limitation because, by definition, the divine both encompasses and exists outside of human reality. The divine is without limits; it is something always to be sought, further up and further in, but never truly found and captured. Although its appearance occurs through human limitation and our experience of it is confined to our human way of understanding, the fact that it even exists at all to the believer as something beyond all shadow and confinement, the fact that our reality owes its existence to

---

80   Eccl. 1:9

the divine, the fact that the divine knows how the human heart is put together because He designed it in the first place, the fact that the author of the divine makes Himself available to those who seek Him, and the fact that He knows every facet of every detail from one end of eternity to the other makes the divine interpretation a good choice for me. I am not in the least discrediting the effort to pursue human knowledge. Being a human myself, I admit that there are rich lessons to be learned here. But once one experiences a fraction of the divine, even for a brief moment, the greatest achievements in this reality appear like dust and ash. As St. Thomas Aquinas observed, "All I have written appears to be as so much straw after the things that have been revealed to me."

Of course, there will be those who disagree with me and that is fine. Faith is something that cannot be proven; it is something that either one has or one does not have. There is no in between. And it is not my responsibility to be the one who parcels it out. I have no interest in that. Each of us chooses a narrative that provides a framework in which to process meaning, interpretation, and understanding in life. Some adopt a religious frame, while others adopt a scientific one. Still others refuse to have anything to do with religion, while others attempt to see the merits of both reason and faith. I take the hybrid approach, attempting to learn as much about human reality through both the lens of faith and the lens of reason. To me, faith and reason are two wings on the same bird; each enriches the other and makes flying anywhere possible. Matters of faith are separate and distinct from matters of reason, and matters of reason should not be explained through faith alone. Even though matters of faith form the ultimate reality, the divine, abdicating human intellect to explain all things through the lens of faith would be a misuse of our human faculties. More to the point, it would be stupid. For this reason, I find it important to dissect human behavior with both a scientific and spiritual scalpel upon a stone table. The discoveries made in one approach tend to fill in the gaps from the other; the subject matter of one is not the subject matter of the other, but the combination of both leads to enriching discussions and discoveries. Faith and reason are meant to complement each other.

Asking a person to choose between faith and reason to the exclusion of the other is like asking a person to choose between the hard sciences or literature to the exclusion of the other. Discoveries made in the hard sciences are not the same as the discoveries illuminated through literature or poetry. One attempts to make sense of the concrete world using observation, measurement, and experimentation through methods of duplicability, reliability, validity, and peer review; the other focuses on the happenings of the interior world, personal observations and reflections, the meaning of the human condition, and the negotiation of emotional, intellectual, or personal conflict. Neither one is "better" than the other. Rather, each has its strengths and weaknesses and its own appropriate time for application. We could describe love in terms of a calculated neurochemical process that occurs in light of childhood impressions within biochemical evolutionary physiology or we could talk about how the heart and soul yearn to have their existence acknowledged before death closes the door within the frame of psychology, philosophy, or spiritual exposition. The "truths" in one do not invalidate the "truths" in the other. Dismissing one as irrelevant or unimportant ignores the wealth of potential information therein and usually has deeper motivations beyond pure epistemology.

If I had to choose between dealing with a person who emphasized reason and minimized faith or a person who minimized reason and emphasized faith, I would choose the former. A common language must be shared between people for them to have any conversation at all. Since faith seems, more often than not, to reflect a personal preference not grounded in reason but in emotion, I find it tedious to interpret other people's frothy and slobbery emotional convictions through a reasonable lens. Undisciplined emotion amplifies emotion and soon there's so much emotional noise that attempting to navigate the complexities of feelings requires more effort than what it is worth. Emotions are a depth without clarity and a power without discipline. The person who relies on their emotions to guide them through life has a poor and tumultuous guide. Feelings often change from one moment to the next and add an element of indiscriminate brutal club swinging to a reasonable exchange; reason, on the other hand, is colder but uses a fencing sword to pinpoint strikes. Emotion is the mountain; reason is the needle. I would rather surround myself with needles who disagree with my opinion than with mountains who cannot see beyond themselves because they are too caught up in themselves.

Ideally, however, I seek out and take pleasure in those like myself who discipline their emotions with reason, those who focus emotional power into a concentrated point, controlling it as best they can in order to produce the effects aligning with conscious choice. Granted, when emotion battles reason, emotion always wins. Emotions reside in the older limbic area of the brain, which evolved both to protect our ancestors from threats and to motivate sexual behavior in order to propagate the species. Reason resides in the prefrontal cortex of the brain, a recent development in our evolution, and makes possible abstract thinking and planning, decision-making, personality regulation, and moderating social behavior. Our emotional brain is older than our reasonable brain, and despite what those frigid reasonable Vulcan types say to the contrary, everyone has emotions. Consciously suppressing them, locking them away, or otherwise ignoring them is not advisable. Emotions generate their own energy and power and if one were to put a "lid" on them, so to speak, pressure would build to the point that the resulting explosion would launch the lid into the air, causing unnecessary chaos. No, it is better to acknowledge emotions, give them a voice, and attempt to discipline them with reason, even if disciplining them means writing a book about the topic as an act of Freudian sublimation.

Anatomically, men and women share more in common than the differences between them. Each differ through their physical accidents, such as genitalia, height, weight, hair, eye, and skin color, and ethnicity. And for the purposes of satisfying evolution's reproductive mandate, one woman is just as good and pleasurable as the next. But in order to solve the loneliness problem, one must look to the differences in the mind and spirit between them. The ideal mate, from my point of view, is one who excites both evolution, the physical and material, and the spirit, the mind and the passions. Most women nowadays focus on one to the detriment of the other; most never find the need or the self-motivation to sharpen their minds to the degree that they sculpt their bodies. One is temporary and the other lasts much longer. Few women dedicate equal effort to mind and spirit; they build enough intellect to control or seduce their mate(s), but never quite enough to inspire him to evolve beyond his intellectual limitations. They remain at, below, or just above his level and never show further interest in chasing wisdom and knowledge for its own sake unless it benefits her selfish desire.

Human beings are either spiritual creatures within the frame of evolutionary biochemistry, biochemical organisms within the realm of the divine, or biochemical organisms in the divine-less material world who create meaning for themselves on their journey toward death. Whichever the case, one must choose a narrative, any narrative, to begin understanding and interpreting the world in order to make sense of things. One needs to begin somewhere with something, anything, in order to have a primordial basis of comparison when new information presents itself. How one goes about creating meaning for themselves reveals their presence in the world and provides a means for others to access them. Choosing a narrative means choosing a value system and adopting the system's hierarchical structure for understanding and classifying information; not choosing or choosing to maintain one's inherited system likewise reveals one's particular interactive methodology.

Everything is information to us. Observers should make every attempt to discover different value systems held by different people and imagine how their choices make sense from within its frame. This ability requires mental flexibility and a certain tolerance for entertaining the contrast between the observer's perspective and the perspective from the observed. The natural attitude for most people caught up in the familiar, those who are not observers themselves but who are instead "participants," is to dismiss contrary or different systems, to engage in an ego competition over who is most "right," and to use these opportunities to bolster what they already believe rather than to identify potential shortcomings and make the necessary modifications to expand consciousness into new horizons of thinking, believing, perceiving, imagining, understanding, and being.

A certain emotional, intellectual, and spiritual "dissection" is required in order to free one from the natural attitude. Until our own preconceptions are challenged with vigor and reason, we have no motivation to see things in the world in a new manner. We could, in theory, challenge ourselves by reading books that we usually do not read or by involving ourselves with people outside of our comfort zone. But if solo effort were so easy and so readily available, then we would expect to see its positive effects in the wider society and culture. But we do not. What we see instead is more of the same: mundane people who mistake good things for bad and bad things for good until they are buried with their regrets. Just as one gains physical strength from interacting with challenging weights, or just as one gains wisdom and knowledge from interacting with difficult ideas, one's value system needs to be stressed and pushed in order to reveal any weaknesses and for it to produce any fruits. Either death will come along and take someone close to us or we fall in love with someone with whom we are receptive to their being in the world. Both instances translate into a profound stimulus and offer the opportunity to transcend limits to the one interested in seeking and asking for such a thing. In any case, the combination of some profound stimulus with the personal desire to use it as a launching point into the unknown is needed before dissection has merit.

More often than not, we meet certain individuals who possess the strengths that we lack and nurture a relationship with them in order to harness their power to make it our own. While it is possible to break free from the natural attitude alone through one's own solo effort, sometimes the process of growth requires the intervention of someone we care about deeply. Emotional, intellectual, and spiritual dissection requires a certain willingness on both the part of the observer and on the part of the observed, as master and apprentice, to engage in the effort together. One is the teacher and the other is the student, at least in the beginning. Later, the student will become the teacher. Each must enter into the power differential relationship willingly and each must not run away from the pain that happens throughout dissection. During this time, the teacher wields the scalpel and, upon a stone table, the apprentice endures the pain of having their habits, preconceptions, familiarities, comforts, thoughts, feelings, and behaviors challenged and ripped away in order for new and better systems to replace them. This is a very intense process and a lot of old feelings and thoughts will float to the surface of consciousness as a consequence. Therefore, it is important for the student to choose a capable teacher who has a clear vision of what is right and good. It is likewise important for the teacher to remain faithful to the greater cause and, to the best of his or her ability, tend to the wounds caused during vulnerable moments.

In all likelihood, sex and sexuality will play a part in this unique relationship as another expression of the shared intimacy, vulnerability, and trust between the two. This should not come as a surprise between a man and a woman, who need little to no excuse for intimacy in the first place. The place of their bodily union is also the gateway for channeling the creation of new souls, hence each is drawn there in the flesh and a certain degree of reverence should accompany their mutual comfort. This is also the reason that undisciplined sexual activity is not recommended for either of them. The more sexual partners a woman has, the less she is able to bond with any one among them,[81] the more she is desensitized to the submission of the act, and the less likely that the teacher's scalpel will penetrate her emotions, intellect, and spirit. Observers, remember Eve's lesson: women submit neither to their God nor to their partner, but only to that which they desire beforehand. If her spirit does not submit to you of her own accord, then all effort with her is a waste of time, and you are serving a function to her well below your talent.

Men should also take heed and limit their physical intimacy with women. A man who leaps from one partner to the next without any

---

81   Better Bachelor. (2020, May 18). *There is a difference between men's and women's casual flings, and science says so.* [Video]. YouTube. https://www.youtube.com/watch?v=488F9P9vZ7c

purpose or direction, or who settles for any woman who falls from the sky into his arms, is a man deceived by and uncertain of his own loneliness. He might know what he wants, but he knows not from whom he wants it because he does not really know himself. This man is more likely to deceive himself that this woman or that woman holds the answer as he is unable to sharpen his intellect and passion. He is like a locksmith with one key but uncertain about the lock for which it was made; the more locks he tries, the more the key's spirit is worn until most of its metal has worn away from repeated insertions and extractions. Should the original lock for which it was designed appear, their key will not be able to unlock it for its shape has changed from the beginning, and rather than forging a new key, he will believe that his worn key is meant for the worn lock. It was easy for Adam to know that Eve was his forever mate because she was literally the only female in existence. But for us, the task is more difficult because we will never know which "Eve" or "Adam" is meant for us unless we probe the issue further.

Let us imagine a scenario where Eve never ate the fruit, never passed it along to Adam, and Lucifer never entered into the equation. While it is true that our fallen efforts to understand events before the fall will be contaminated with sin, and will therefore be imperfect, the human mind might still be able to glean a portion of God's original plan for man and woman with grace. Both man and woman were made for one another after God had made each of them for Himself; He intended for both of them to keep their eyes fixed upon Him throughout their development and unquestionably follow Him first and foremost. They were to pursue Him, each in their own way, and as a result, grow closer together themselves. Imagine a triangle with point A, E, and G. The base of the triangle is composed of two points, A and E. The head of the triangle has one point, G. Adam travels along line AG, moving closer to G. Eve travels along line *EG* and moves closer to *G*. The closer that Adam and Eve move toward *G* because of their own effort, the closer the distance between *AG* and *EG*.

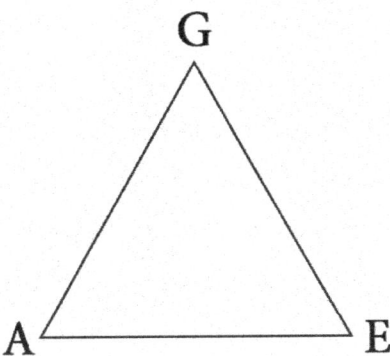

The problem pre-fall and post-fall is that *A* focuses on *E* to the exclusion of *G*, and *E* focuses on *A* to the exclusion of *G*. Or rather, *A* takes *E* to be *G* and *E* takes *A* to be *G*. *E* implements certain tactics to beckon *A* hither and *A* has his own strategies of luring *E* closer. Line *AE* has been explored thoroughly to the point of boredom, as there is nothing new under the sun concerning the things men and women do together. Every orifice has been filled. Every sweet nothing has been spoken. All that is "new" is the reincarnation of orgasms at different moments in time.

Therefore, dear observer, I tell you in truth, *A* must seek *E* who first seeks *G* and *E* must seek *A* who first seeks *G*. Each must be motivated in themselves to pursue the greater good alone; *A* and *E* should encounter one another in the process of each seeking, asking, and knocking toward *G*. And once *A* and *E* discover one another, and a universe manifests between them, both of them continue on their travel toward *G* together, never reaching it, but always looking for it, moving closer to it, both together and separately. Now, for those who have no faith in the divine but rely on reason alone, *G* is not necessarily God, although from my point of view, all truth, wisdom, and holiness, wherever it be found, flows from Him. *G* is "reason" dwelling beyond limitation and habitual perception, imperceptible until desire uncovers the tunnel or softens the wall leading toward it; it is wisdom, honor, truth, discipline, focus, and harmony between body, soul, and mind. The path toward *G* demands ever more clarity in understanding, interpreting, and communicating in proportion to the distance traveled toward it inward and upward. Clinging to the pursuit of *G* means taking personal responsibility, changing and refining habits when needed, continually evolving from one moment to the next, and accepting the possibility that either *A* or *E* might be lost in the journey. I call the people who chase after *G* "truth seekers."

Truth seekers, more often than not, begin as low-status socially rejected and undesirable males who possess an inquisitive nature. They may or may not adopt a religious narrative with faith, but certainly start with a foundation based in reason and logic. Cliques tend to avoid them at all stages of development from childhood to adulthood for their withdrawn silence and social awkwardness, lack of discernible traits or resources, and their inability to conform to the whims of the social environment. They tend to favor solitude instead of gatherings of people, derive pleasure from contemplating abstract ideas as opposed to sensory stimuli, suppress their emotions or show them to very few trusted individuals, but often pen their emotions to paper, and like to take decisive action rather than get lost considering possibilities. They recognize that most people are innately chaotic, hostile, lustful, animalistic, unstable, or deceptive and preempt any interaction with them by locking away their emotions and hiding their important thoughts and insights with either silence or feigned ignorance. Truth seekers tend to excel in academic matters and take pride in their studies and drink the attention from teachers and from others in positions of power who recognize their intellectual abilities and talents. They hold disdain for stimulants and depressants and those who indulge in them to excess as they believe that drugs interfere with internal harmony and the exactness of thoughts and feelings. From their point of view, weakness, lack of motivation and discipline, and hedonism drive those who indulge in drugs or narcotics. It is as if truth seekers were born to seek deeper understanding, clarity of perception, and knowledge and wisdom, regardless of where it dwells. If they were not born to it, their innate curiosity leads them to question traditional societal totems and taboos and "acceptable" expressions of affection. Above all else, they desire to uncover and understand the logical system binding people and ideas together.

Pain creates truth seekers. It is not as if truth seekers lack all emotion; in fact, passion motivates them as much as logic does. Trauma, abandonment, being misunderstood, frustration, injustice, anger, sadness, and emotional chaos force them to recluse into themselves for their own protection, like a turtle, adopt an *introverted* orientation, and learn to observe people and situations from afar in order to avoid and to decipher the innate pain flowing from other people, especially from those whose duty it was to care for them the most. The greatest defense to chaos, they reason, is to avoid troublesome situations altogether, if not through physical absence, then through intellectual and emotional absence.

Like all humans, they want to feel comforted, want to surrender themselves to the warmth of an embrace, want to feel someone's gentle fingers stroke their hair, and derive emotional satisfaction through the five senses but they cannot. Over time, they learned that harboring such wants inevitably leads to pain. Others taught them that bad things follow good things and that good things are unreliable, insincere, and short-lived.

Therefore, they create a version of external reality inside themselves and would rather interact with their created derivative than expose themselves to real chaos and instability. For this reason, they are more *intuitive* than sensory. This is the safest course of action, they reason, that allows them to interact with the exterior world in a controlled manner.

Emotions, to them, are inconsistent, unreliable, fleeting, and always lead to pain, loneliness, and suffering. They have seen the fruit of undisciplined minds from those who worship emotions and perceive them as petty and child-like tyrants, regardless of their gender, age, or status. Those who submit to such a ruler cannot themselves be logical, but rather instinctual, and are likely to change feelings without a moment's notice—their consistency rests in their inconsistency, and truth seekers believe that logical consistency is a prerequisite for stability. They do not put their faith in any individual person but in the logical systems motivating that person. They interpret the emotions as powerful yet chaotic, unpredictable, and risky. They are aware of their own emotions too and refuse to allow them to have control and exert monumental amounts of internal energy to keep their inner demons chained to the wall. Therefore, truth seekers derive comfort from abstracting and translating emotion into intellect and value *thinking* over feeling.

Nothing described thus far matters without decisive action. If the truth seeker is wrong, he or she will learn about their error only after enacting their strategies, plans, and beliefs. Should an error rise to the surface as a consequence, the truth seeker will refine their craft in such a manner that prevents future errors of the same. They disdain inaction in order to contemplate the numerous possibilities feeding into antecedents and consequences. For them, moving from one rabbit hole of thought to the next is akin to spinning on a merry-go-round, in that both provide the illusion of movement without getting any closer to the destination. For truth seekers, all that matters is the goal regardless of the manner to obtain it. For this reason, truth seekers value *judging* over perceiving.

There are fewer female truth seekers than male truth seekers, not because there are fewer women than men in the world as both exist in similar numbers, but because there is less incentive for women to exert the effort needed to be a seeker in the first place. High-value males, with easier access to pleasure and distraction due to genetics or to wealth and resources, also lack the incentive to process emotional trauma in creative ways. The prerequisites for this particular kind of being in the world is pain, rejection, loneliness, frustration, and social isolation. Women experience these negative things too, to be sure, but evolution provides them with inherent seduction and secrets as a quick and easy way to negotiate them. Men, on the other hand, cannot wear short skirts, show cleavage, adorn themselves with fishnets and high heels, post pictures of their flesh online, and use enhancing cosmetics with the conclusive expectation to exploit women due to their inherent hunger for sex. This is how women exploit men. Men with few other options use their intellect to combat emotional pain and are more likely to become truth seekers as they age. Women do not inherently desire sex to the same degree that men do and are therefore less prone to delight in the raw and visceral distraction it provides; women, with less testosterone and more secrets to protect, use sex as a tool to seduce the men they want. Although they derive a degree of pleasure from the activity, pleasure for its own sake is not their goal. Their goal is to reap the intangible benefit from men that it provides. It is easier for them to hide from the pain than to confront it. Men, especially adolescent males, do not have this picking-and-choosing luxury and must therefore find other ways to conquer the pain.

When presented with negative experience, women have the ready option to distract themselves with sexual relations with a man—any man. Women offer their bodies as an amusement park and do not need intellectual talents, high status, or the drive toward continual self-improvement to attract visitors; youth, beauty, and fertility are all that are needed, and it is a shame if that is all she has.

Those women who fail to attach themselves to a potential or actual truth seeker settle for beta male providers who find complete content with nothing more than the sex she parcels out as he possesses no further drive to explore the complicated systems of logic motivating both his and her behavior. Women who partner up with weak men need legions of "friends" to provide her with what her beta cannot. If you are such a man, now you know why your woman indulges in social media, posts pictures of herself, and entertains multiple men through "friendly" text conversation. If you were all she needed and wanted, as she says, then other men would never pick up the breadcrumbs she drops because she would not drop them in the first place. Plausible deniability will scream "platonic" while evolution whispers something else. Now ask yourself, is the juice worth the squeeze?

Dear observer, let us synthesize our discussion thus far and alter our perceptual lens in light of the concepts described. Much of what is written in this book passed at least twice through my perceptual lens: first through experience and second through articulation. As I write and rewrite, always searching for better clarity to avoid potential misinterpretation and misunderstanding, the concepts and words under scrutiny continue to pass back and forth through my lens, solidifying my penmanship and involvement, imbuing my soul into these words and topics presented for your consideration. In order to strengthen our bond together as teacher and student and to clear the path forward between us, I wanted to lay my mind naked before you and describe my biases in a forthright manner, providing you with threads, breadcrumbs, data points, and fruits on purpose that could help you find me if you desired to seek me out. Through the things I write and through the manner I present them, you have come to know me and are able to choose to submit to my scalpel while laying upon my stone table.

When humanity fell from grace, Lucifer claimed equal parentage with God and forever bound his essence to our own, marring God's breath of life within us and forever binding us with our own hands to sin, lust, and death.[82] The story of Adam and Eve repeats to this day; everyone who draws breath dies and everyone who pursues the good inevitably deals with darkness. God is love.[83] How are we, the descendants of the fallen, to find compatible mates, love, and purpose when they walked with Love, talked with Love, and owed their existence to Love but still rejected it? How are we, the sinful, to succeed when they, the sinless, failed?

The answer rests in our response to loneliness. Man and woman have been chasing one another since Eden, mistaking each other for the greater good, attempting to seduce and lure one another closer to themselves for consumption, and seeing the other as the missing puzzle piece within. Their shortcomings grew from idolizing pleasures and resources extracted from the other, wanting and believing that something temporary is permanent. Only after each seeks, asks, knocks, and desires toward reasonable things or divine things in their solitude will a genuine encounter with the other become possible. Men, in their loneliness, must seek greater reason. Women, in their solitude, must petition reason for

---

82   Jn. 8:44

83   1 Jn. 4:8

purpose and meaning. This entails using a spiritual scalpel to remove the emotional cancer filling the inner hollow, and if one is unable, unwilling, or unsure how to do this on their own, then they must submit themselves to a loving teacher, who is a doctor of sorts, who acts in the best interests of the seeker. Whether alone or with the aid of someone else, it is up to each individual to submit, to desire, and to be open to the greater.

One does not necessarily have to "believe" in the Judeo-Christian narrative in order to move forward. A "reason" interested in pursuing truth and love is enough in the beginning stages. All inquisitive minds, otherwise known as truth seekers, are welcome at our table. A reasonable believer and a faithful scientist or a reasonable scientist and a faithful believer should agree on enough to start the journey as both seek deeper truth, clarity, understanding, wisdom, and aspire to evolve beyond limitation. While each focus on different subject matters, i.e., the material versus the divine, each proceeds with human reason, the common language spoken among truth seekers.

Let us, once again, turn our attention to the man and woman sitting at that table in the nightclub. The genesis for my disdain and contempt for them rests in their participation in the eternal repetition of the same: A to E not G, E to A not G, EA and AE without G. The desires of their heart find fulfilment in one another first, like Adam and Eve did toward one another, whereas my teacher said, "Set your hearts on his kingdom first, and on God's saving justice, and all these other things will be given you as well."[84] This means that when A and E, in silence and solitude, seek G, then both A and E will discover one another through their effort finding G.

---

84   Mt. 6:33

Observe the manner of her clothes and see how she leverages evolution's gift to her advantage; witness how he responds to her siren's call, takes pride in his ability to bed the mark using this strategy or that, and desires the pleasure of her mouth or between her legs more than he desires the fruit of reason, much less the fruit of faith. Hundreds of years ago, a similar man who chased lust in his youth observed in his later years, "Thou hast made us for thyself, O Lord, and our heart is restless until it finds its rest in thee."[85] The games men and women play with each other are born from loneliness and express themselves as restlessness.

---

85   Augustine, S. (1961). *Confessions* (New impression ed.). Penguin Classics.

> **"**
>
> *Iron is sharpened by iron,*
> *one person is sharpened by contact*
> *with another.*
>
> —*Proverbs 27:17*

FRACTIONS OF WHETSTONES

We have walked together this far, dear observer, and I ask that you tolerate my company a little longer. The time given to me to be with you draws closer to the end, but we are not yet at the destination of my design where the distance traveled between us makes sense in retrospect. While you and I may not share the same narrative, we share the same intellect and reason upon which all narratives are built. But reason alone cannot explain what motivates me to put pen to paper or finger to keyboard, exposing my soul to you through written words; it is love. Love is the hidden thread binding these words together, the unseen motivation behind my intellect, and my desire to press forward. I wanted to tell you this here, now, because tomorrow is not guaranteed, and I have seen for myself how people are here one minute and are gone the next. I do not want to leave here knowing that I left words unspoken or feelings unexpressed under lock and key. I would rather regret the things I have done and said than the things not done and not said.

I feel compelled, you see, to follow my master's order.[86] He does not coerce me to do so nor do I feel that I act out of my indebtedness to his teaching. Neither guilt nor fear require love from me. Rather, some part of me changed during my walk with Him and the time I spent contemplating His words, and though I still perceive myself as wretched, I know He sees me as something else—something that I cannot see in myself through myself. He overfills my cup and I feel a certain sense of duty to pour the blessings I receive from Him into those willing to receive it from me.[87] To Him, I have value and I still have a role to play within His grand design. When He asked me to feed His sheep, I wanted to comply and do so, imperfectly, in a nontraditional manner according to what I thought was best at the time.[88] Sometimes, my intervention caused more harm than good and at other times, others accepted my gift and became better people as a result. Therefore, it is my hope that my words find you, dear observer, well. And if my words have no effect upon you, then at least use them as a stepping stone to find answers elsewhere. You must seek the truth, even if that seeking means departing from me.

He showed me that I am His whetstone and that my special talent rests in sharpening blades.[89] It is for me to neither forge nor build, to

---

86   Jn. 21:15-17

87   Ps. 23:5

88   Jn. 21:15-17

89   Prv. 27:17

neither heal nor comfort, and to neither inspire nor prophesy, but to grind away dullness through abrasive pain, subtle and overt, in order to prepare axes, swords, daggers, and arrows for battle. Sometimes weak metal breaks and sometimes stubborn metal does not yield to the process but every woman who passes across my stone and submits to its purpose always leaves sharper and better than before our paths crossed.

Along with feminine blades, there are feminine grinding rocks. Though I did not realize it at the time it was happening during my youth, all the various love pains and negative relationship experiences in my life that influenced me to become a truth seeker were the rocks grinding against *my* rock, spirit against spirit, gradually shaping me into a multi-faceted whetstone capable of putting an edge on most blades. Some rocks were coarse grit and simply emotional, while others were fine grit and encompassed both passion and intellect. Both the pain and my response to it shaped the perceptual lens I continue to use to this day, and though I did not understand why I had to endure the things I did long ago, now in retrospect, it makes sense and the love I once cursed now enables me to sharpen others.

From the timeless perspective of the divine, certain events needed to happen at certain times in my life in order to push my spirit this way or that way. Looking back on it all, there was an unseen reason behind all my intimate interactions with females. However, the divine's fore-knowledge does not imply predestination, as our prior knowledge of the sun rising and setting does not itself cause the Earth to rotate. In other words, even though God knew the consequence of my free will prior to its enactment, He caused neither me nor the girls in my life to follow a predetermined script for them to become rocks or blades. Rather, I chose to interpret events in my life in a certain manner, to rebel against some ideas while embracing others, and to accept certain outcomes while denying others. I've been a whetstone all along, but never understood myself as one until quite recently. Free will animates all I have done and all that has been done to me. God knew the future in the past, I did not. To me, each interaction back then was unique and new, full of wonder and excitement.

Throughout my relationships with them, I kept close to the divine, churning his words over and over again in my heart, and in my own clumsy yet well-intention way, I prayed for Him to show me the way throughout, His way, and to place my footsteps in His during my life-long journey toward Him. I, too, am legion with both my love of God and my love of women swarming in my heart. Since adolescence, I have kept private the relationship between myself and the divine, revealing fragments of it to a few here and there according to their comfort level and according to my clarity and understanding of it at the time. But now, with this writing, I step out of the cave into the sun to share that which I hold to be most precious with those who have ears to hear it.

In my middle age, being a "whetstone" now symbolizes how I interpret my core self to exist within intimate relationships, whether physical, spiritual, emotional, intellectual, or some combination of all four. Either I sharpen blades or others grind themselves against me, enhancing my stone with heartbreak and eventual disappointment. These two modalities, rock and blade or teacher and student, characterize why others draw me closer to themselves and why I draw others closer to myself; it also describes our mutual purpose in the ebb and flow of the nuance between us.

Looking back across the history of my intimacy with women from middle age reveals two distinct patterns in my youth: I approached rocks;

blades approached me. That is, when I sought intimacy from women, they always turned out to be rocks, pleasurable but ultimately disappointing, although to them, I owe a great debt. Without their pain, I would have never grown. When women sought me out and accepted intimacy from me, they were the blades, upon whom I did my best work. Never did a woman announce herself to me as a rock or blade in the beginning, for few know themselves well enough in their youth. Now I know that they can be both blade and rock simultaneously, depending upon their submission or obstinance to the man they are with; contemplation in retrospect upon my pursuit of them or upon their pursuit of me made their purpose within my tapestry clear. Women either accepted or rejected submission to me and, by extension, to the love imbued in my whetstone; they, not I, made themselves rocks or blades, but all of them wore my rock, my spirit, over time into a whetstone, a special rock meant to sharpen blades and grind new whetstones.

Rocks perceive and interact with me differently than blades, as the former tend to be guarded, opaque, and narcissistic. They feast upon the energy and attention I invest into the relationship, but fail, more often than not, to reciprocate in both degree and kind. They seek me out not for insight but for distraction or for comfort through distraction. They ask me for various favors: to help move their furniture, to assist with a financial shortcoming, or to listen to their dramatic stories filled with conflict and competition with an understanding ear biased toward their side of the story. They never seem to accept the wisdom of my words or recognize the compassion behind my interactions with them or do so half-heartedly; when they do recognize it, they rarely reciprocate it to the same extent, acknowledging my contribution, my wisdom, and my emotion with a simple "thanks," as if everything I do with them was just as meaningful as loaning them a cheap pencil and a few sheets of paper for art class.

They volunteer showing me fractions of their pain and brokenness, both provoking my sympathy and creating a special space for me inside their heart to dwell as the hero, savior, or knight in shining armor. Both they and I know that I possess unique blessings, talents, strengths, and insights uncommon among men yet they still restrict my movement within their heart and mind, citing one excuse or another to keep me motionless within themselves, a trinket of affection placed alongside others in their emotional trophy case of adoring suitors. Wringing me tight as a wet sponge in order to extract as much water from me as possible happens more often than not. I quench their thirst for a short time, but shortly afterwards I am thanked, dismissed, and forgotten. Rescuing them from the brink of spiritual dehydration is commonplace, or so it seems, as I am left to recharge my nourishment with "thanks." Such women take for granted discovering my hidden water well in the desert of life, finding respite with me for a brief moment on their journey toward another man whose water is not as pure or refreshing. Their vulnerable moments during these times are few and far between, made even sweeter to me by the passing hours or days, yet those moments end up feeling artificial and calculated, adding a few extra drops of fuel to a sputtering interaction.

For example, on one occasion, a rock described repeated incidents of early-adolescent sex abuse from an older male; she was a young teen and he was in his mid-twenties, for such raw disclosure reflected the "comfort" between us. She revealed her continued naïve passionate involvement with him over the following years as a family friend, and, after they were over, his condemnable behavior for initiating and continuing the carnal relationship during her youth. In her adulthood, years after her abuser left, during her reflection with me, she was drawn to remember the romps of her youth when an intimate relationship ended or when her current intimate involvements seemed unsure. Because she knew my disposition toward care, concern, and empathy beforehand, my inevitable response to her various pains, traumas, and discomforts was predictable and served to soften any personal objection I had to the distance forming between us. It is as if she knew how portraying herself as a weak, vulnerable, and damaged victim would affect me. I cared for her deeply, and she knew it and exploited it, lapping up the positive energy flowing through my cold water while contributing nothing but an empty cup.

Words given to me were meant to translate her reluctance, elicit forgiveness, and produce a predetermined response, not to move the conversational intimacy between us forward in a meaningful and lasting way. I would come to learn that after our talks together about topics general and personal, she would find satisfaction in another's company, casually appreciating my effort with "thanks" in her eager stride toward him and his single-minded carnal goal. She emptied his passionate overflowing "cup" for the night and took empowering delight in sedating the wild beast with her pleasure. The brokenness she described to me failed to attract her contemplation in solitude, as was my first advice; instead, she leveraged my tender reaction to halt my intellectual advancement upon her heart in order to advance herself toward a legion of men less worthy. The childhood trauma that stopped her spiritual intimacy with me was not an issue when it came for her to be physically intimate with others. To the one who cared about her, she made rules, but to the ones who could care less about her, she made exceptions. When she moved away from me, she was in her early twenties and I fear my words will not reach her ears and heart until she reaches her mid-thirties after her youth is over. One day, perhaps she will find a beta man to clean up what other men left so messy and force him to pay for something that legions of others got for free. This is the look of modern love and why I passionately objected to the man and woman sitting at that table in the nightclub—each broken themselves, but wanting the other to repair their broken with the broken through the broken for the purpose of mending. How absurd.

Rocks differ from one another and in that difference, some possess a finer grit than others. You see, most feminine rocks are coarse and rough, ruled by their passions and by their seeking of validation. Infatuated by their own beauty and by their power to hypnotize the weak-minded, most rocks are content to roll from one place to another with no real direction guiding their path. They wash themselves in the ocean of compliments gifted from thirsty men; few among them ever become bona fide whetstones, for only an intellectual predisposition rooted in divine command that tempers the emotions create whetstones. For rocks, there are many alternatives to meditating upon pain and suffering as they reflexively and instinctually entertain many pleasant distractions through their flesh. Most women are coarse rocks and replicants, nothing more, and do not even realize it because "passion and emotion" feels better than "logic and truth." Frustration and disappointment left in their wake grind away soft hearts and encourage men to build walls, withdraw into themselves, reject emotion, rely on intelligence, adopt pessimism, and accept loneliness and solitude.

Men who adopt a religious narrative will feel the most conflicted emotional turmoil and inner conflict with common rocks. On the one hand, they are told that God loves everyone, and that if they truly love God, then they will love their neighbor as themselves after loving God with all their heart, mind, and soul.[90] On the other hand, they must consider the fruit of pain that loving rocks bring, the bitter reward for vulnerability, truth, and honesty, and figure out how to balance genuine love of God with love for his fellow human being in the face of being hurt by the ones he has been commanded to love. To sharpen the point further, divine command requires that primordial whetstones love their God, love themselves, and love the ones who hurt him. Whetstones are forced to negotiate this apparent contradiction and must resolve the tension between passion, intellect, and spirit in a reasonable manner.

Most men are naïve and some among them choose to keep falling in love, over and over, until finally no hurt originates from the woman he loves. These men willingly expose their heart to the whims of others and believe that their endurance will be rewarded. He is willing to suffer under the feminine lash, indefinitely, accepting its bite and disappointment for love's sake in search of emotional and spiritual peace and quiet, a return to childlike innocence and unconditional love from mother, the male–mother bond.[91] It is not that this man ever grew wiser, better, and stronger and learned from the pain. It is just that he persisted through the pain from various women until at last finding and latching onto the first one who did not hurt him. He is proud to call this one "wife." To build a relationship upon masculine weakness, with the feminine "acceptance" of this weakness, is like building a house on sand.[92] They may comfort one another for a time, but the day will come when he reaps the reward from avoiding confronting his deep need to seek female validation. The fruits of understanding differ from the fruits of ignorance.

---

90   Mt. 22:36-40

91   Psych2Go. (2018, September 4). *6 types of unhealthy mother son relationships* [Video]. YouTube. https://www.youtube.com/watch?v=uz8sJ0ZNxUA

92   Mt. 7:26

Other men internalize the pain, unable to process it all at once, and carry it with them into the future for further analysis. It grinds upon their heart and mind long after its creator departs from his presence. These men are determined to dissect the pain, understand it, and figure out how to leverage its lessons to increase their wisdom, but lack the training to do so in the acute moment. They struggle with the emotional pain, sometimes for years, seeking understanding and asking for wisdom and discernment. They learn about themselves through the pain, with the pain, and because of the pain and use their anger and frustration to fuel their journey along the unknown path in order to overcome the inner weakness that made possible the pain in the first place. With gradual intelligence and divine assistance, they step out onto an unseen path with faith. Loneliness is their companion and solitude is their guide. From these men, whetstones are born.

"Pain is proportional to the degree of masculine surrender to the feminine," new whetstones reckon. "Adam was made to lead Eve, to inspire her surrender and be worthy of her submission;[93] disorder and chaos came about when Adam instead surrendered his will to her and ate the fruit she presented. His fear of a life without Eve was stronger than his trust in God. And all of his sons since inherited his original weakness," they conclude. "If Eve rejected God's law and Adam's rule, elevating her desire above both, submitting herself to the object of her desire rather than to the good and perfect laid at her feet within her grasp, then what chance do the fallen sons of Adam have to inspire submission in the fallen daughters of Eve?" they contemplate. "The only real power women have over men is found in men's desire for them, within their inheritance of Adam's original yearning for Eve in general and in their

---

93   Eph. 5:22-25

desire for pleasures of her flesh in particular. For what power would a woman have with no feminine endowments, no genitalia, no fertility, no beauty, no youth, and no comfort? She would not be a woman at all; no man would pay her attention unless her mind inspired otherwise, and even so, such attention would be limited to intellectual stimulation with zero eroticism. What would her seduction be if all her seductions were cast into the void?" they question.

However, there are some women predisposed toward logic and truth, but their numbers are few. Their mental training usually begins before adolescence, a discipline lovingly taught by their mother and father through example, at a time well before discovering the power and allure of their sexuality, setting the background against which their physical maturity will eventually unfold. One or both of her parents are usually whetstones themselves, with a career in or at least a fond attachment to philosophy or some other academic discipline, which their daughter imitates like the infant's tongue. The love and attention they bestow upon her intertwines with their love for mind and spirit, and she drinks it in and makes it a part of herself. Upon this foundation, she begins to build initial perceptions of the world.

Wisdom and love nourish her both through her parents and apart from her parents. Her parents impress upon her from a young age to read various books, engage in difficult conversations about ideas and the themes therein, and they provide depth, context, and guidance to her budding mind. She is both a daughter and a willing and curious student. During puberty, testosterone does not boil her blood with rage and desire, though through observation, she is very much aware of the relational dynamics between males and females. Religion and/or the quest for wisdom and understanding disciplines and tempers her carnal desire and she would rather read stories about romance and about the human heart than to adopt a romance for herself. When the time comes that she enters into a relationship, she finds herself deciphering both herself and her mate through the wisdom of the treasured authors who described movements of the heart. Those she keeps in her legion are all seeking greater wisdom and insight for themselves; she only accepts and allows seeds from her parent's passion tree to grow in her personal life; the man whom she will ultimately love will mirror her father's and mother's mind, wisdom, and discipline.

As a young woman, she walks with depression and loneliness, as most intellectuals do, a malady caused by too much awareness that more often than not desires either religious submission or self-medication, for example, drugs and alcohol, to dampen or reassure the mind; she spends time apart from her parents learning about herself and her passions and she realizes that the number of men who share her appreciation, inspiration, passion, and discipline, who are either her equal or superior, are few and far between. She inspires most men but is not inspired by them, enriches them but is not enriched by them, guides them but is not guided by them, and sharpens them but is not sharpened by them. Her ideal standard of a man is somewhat of a Frankenstein creation formed by her combining the best parts of the imagination from the many different authors who wrote about love and the human heart. She desires a man with the mind of a philosopher, the heart of a poet, the spirit of a saint, and the compassion of her parents, but, in her youth, cannot find one who stands apart from among her peers. She feels alone and misunderstood and this frustrates her. A book cannot warm her bed; the endearments passed between two fictional characters leaves her yearning for something similar. Imagination cannot replace a beating heart; a great chasm separates passion written from passion experienced.

The best option among her friends and acquaintances lack at least one of the four—a philosophical mind, a poetic heart, parental compassion, or a saintly spirit—and she feels it her duty to grind against her partner's weakest point(s) in order to determine his merit and improve upon his shortcomings. To her, men are the blades and she is the whetstone. She substitutes submission to a superior intellect with fertilizing a suitor's minds. To enter into an imbalanced relationship with her means laying on her stone table, yielding to her spiritual and intellectual scalpel, and having all irrationalities and unreasonable attachments surgically removed, dissected, and examined. From her point of view, she shows love by grinding away weakness in order for polished strength hidden underneath to shine forth; she would not invest so much of herself unless motivated by a deeper passion, a common trait shared among all whetstones regardless of gender, a trait unappreciated and unperceived by lesser minds who stand to lose all means of life support after the removal of cancerous defects.

Despite their rarity, female whetstones and rocks share a few things in common. After all, one is just a polished and more durable version of the other. Whereas the search for validation through physical stimulation motivates one, the search for meaning and inspiration through intellectual connection motivates the other. Both will never "really" submit to those whom they perceive as weaker than themselves, whether sexually or intellectually, despite numerous prior sexual or conversational engagements with them indicating the contrary. Each carries a depressing or anxious weight, sees dissatisfaction around every corner, and finds ultimate peace and delight within their own imagination. For both, during moments of physical intimacy, the act of penetration is not so much an accepting of the other's soul in physical form into their own body as it is a masturbating with the other's warm tangible parts. One knows the object of searching, but cannot find it; the other does not know for what they are searching, and finds a hollow everything else everywhere else. Both arrange male suitors into hierarchies, never disclosing their exact position to any among them, use replicants to explore the possibilities with those in the friend zone, and are well aware of evolution's mandate to procreate. They differ in the finesse of the execution but achieve the same evolutionary goal, namely, seduction. Both are useful insofar as they grind at different spiritual aspects of men; common rocks produce generalized frustration and grind at the passions alone; female whetstones inspire particular awareness of personal deficits and grind at both the passions and the intellect.

All men will encounter the common rock, few men will ever encounter, much less grind against, a female whetstone for these emerge only under certain uncommon conditions, such as a value system that pursues intellect and reason over emotion, a value system that mandates emotion be processed through sharp reason, a religious or spiritual orientation that observes the sanctity of the individual human soul, and caring and nurturing parents who set the example for seeking the good, asking for grace, and knocking on the doors of long dead intellectuals who dedicated their lives in pursuit of the same.

Most rocks, on the other hand, come from dysfunctional homes with one or both parents emotionally volatile, spiritually crippled, or intellectually stunted. Such parents provide neither inspiration nor guidance because they themselves do not know either; their children, my rocks, do unto me what has been done unto them, and unless the rocks allow me into their minds and hearts, they are fated to pass along their deficient lessons to their children as well. Remember my earlier lesson, "A consciousness that attempts to perceive itself through itself with itself both overlooks and compounds the flaws woven into itself." Extending this logic to the human heart reads as follows: relationships that begin as a consequence of pain, that seek to escape the pain, find the other through pain, need the other to be stronger than their pain in order for them to be able to dissect the pain. The men she chooses to love are born from her emotional pain; pain allows these men to come into focus, and she believes that "loving them" will help her "love herself." However, lesser men will compound her pain because they are bound as a function of it and they will be forever grateful to have her in her brokenness because they themselves lack standards. If sex could have fixed her pain, she would have been fixed many times over by now. Men found through pain and kept sedate with sex have no incentive to evolve. Either through effort and mental discipline, he will seek to understand pain or through passive acceptance, he will seek to be sexually sedated because of it. The man she chooses reflects the woman she is and wants to become. She often deludes herself with their potential to become a great man; if he was truly a great man, she would have encountered him during his own masculine evolution. His effort to improve himself would have carried over to her and would have provided her with inspiration to embark on her journey. But more often than not, she finds and settles for a male version of herself, allowing her temporary peace because each shares the same weaknesses and vices, for example, mutual drug use, alcohol abuse, codependence, anxieties, depressions, and a heavy reliance on sexual expression. Boring. Predictable.

More often than not, common women never achieve the status of whetstone, not because they are incapable, but because they spend much of their effort distracting themselves, avoiding pain and seeking pleasure according to instinctual drive. They do not follow a contemplative life. Women know, especially in their youth, what men want from them, and rather than manipulating men's desire to inspire them to become better men, they leap from one to the next after growing bored of the lesser and inferior, leaving them to seek out the greater and superior. These women do not know how to be alone—in fact, they fear loneliness and solitude the most—and never seek G for the fruits of G are not immediate and apparent, but grow over time like a seed in the earth. They have no incentive to rehabilitate the souls of broken men, to become his muse, to inspire him onward and upward. She does not even know how to fix her own brokenness! She uses mediocre "love" as a Band-Aid to patch cracked bones and internal bleeding! If she knew how to fix herself, she would have done so already and in her wholeness, would have never settled for a weak and broken man in the first place.

Broken women attract broken men and vice versa, and the two comfort each other according to their limited nature and limited abilities. Perhaps she knows that he is damaged beyond her skill level and never bothers to remove his emotional and mental cancer because she cannot recognize it—even if she did, she possesses neither the skill nor the tool to remove it and therefore "nurses" it. Perhaps she finds personal meaning and purpose keeping him in place, attending to him in his lowliness, feeling empowered by her clever sedation of him as she continues dispensing warm and pleasurable "remedies." The meaning she creates for herself grounds itself in the pleasure he extracts from her during orgasmic delight, E to A but not G, and a series of pauses between orgasms measures the tempo of their relationship together.

If he was truly a good man, she would make evident his goodness through her action and word, as a student carries and manifests their teacher's lessons. But her actions and words in secret describe all we need to know about his quality to her. If he satisfied her mind and heart, she would not seek out other minds and hearts.

Knowledgeable and capable women, on the other hand, never bother lowering their standards in the first place; this is why most men never encounter female whetstones—most men are not at their level and are therefore unworthy of her consideration. Broken men glimpse their power and majesty on occasion but intimidation chases them away; men fumble around women with strong intellect. Few ships find safe passage through the sharp rocks protecting her island; only another whetstone treads her waters without fear. Whereas a common man sees such a woman as out of his league, a whetstone simply sees a smart and interesting woman who stands to benefit from his involvement with her if her eyes are willing to see and her ears are willing to hear. All women, whetstone and rock alike, possess dozens of better options in their friendship cage; from their perspective, they could either spend time with one lowly man who fears them or who feels unworthy to be with them or simply make themselves available to all men whom they perceive as stronger than themselves and choose the best option from among the many. She may beckon a weak man due to her emotional disfigurement in the beginning, but as she heals, she will leave him if he does not evolve along with her. Some might argue that it is in her best interest to remain in the familiar as a beautiful cripple. It is easier after all and she can entertain the best of both worlds.

A relationship with a whetstone begins like any other. We laugh, enjoy each other's company, drink, eat, watch movies, and discuss ideas and concepts. All the while during the safe and mundane interactions, we are taking mental notes, collecting data points and breadcrumbs, extrapolating to the value system behind the responses, and evaluating whether or not the other person is worthy of a true investment. We may test the relational waters by throwing out an outlandish or controversial topic in order to see how the other responds to it. We might act out in bizarre or erratic ways on purpose for the same reason. Everything that the other person does or says in response is information to us. Since we make all of our decisions based on information, either we collect what the person offers from afar through observation or we craft scenarios where the other person acts out in closer proximity.

All the information that they provide enables us to identify the rocks from blades and a careful thematic analysis of their responses to previous stimuli suggests their future responses to deeper conversation. At this point, we have invested little of our true nature into the relationship. After interpreting and confirming signals from the blade, we delve into intimacy and we talk about guarded, secret, shameful, guilty, and "inappropriate" things. Sometimes, whetstones assist blades in putting thoughts and ideas into words and model the intellectual and emotional behavior expected in the relationship. Other times, whetstones simply create a safe environment free from stigma and judgment and allow the blade to express herself. We acknowledge their pain when it presents itself, offer alternative interpretations to long-held beliefs when relevant, and inspire them to understand themselves and their motives with reason and logic.

Rocks to others are blades to me when she advances upon me, or rather, when she allows me to advance upon her. Rare is the woman who pursues the man with clear verbal intent. These women, most women, rather drop breadcrumbs of affection and evaluate the man's response. Her test means to measure a man's confidence, strength, and power. As we test her with exaggerated behavior and ideas, she tests us. She guards herself throughout with plausible deniability, as all women do, and to the one from whom she wants intimacy, she accepts. To the one whom she does not want, she rejects and explains that her breadcrumbs are just one big misunderstanding. It is the women, not I, who decide to become rocks or blades.

Rocks never submit to me and my method, whereas blades do. Submission is always their choice and is necessary before moving forward. Blades learn to trust me over time and understand that any painful grinding comes from a place of betterment with the explicit purpose of sharpening their edge long after our time together ends. We begin intimacy with mutual vulnerability by exchanging childhood stories, historical recountings of pivotal moments that shaped our attitude, or through discussing personal opinions on matters near and dear to our hearts, including religion and spirituality, the nature of love, and what it means to be human. The subject of conversation is not as important as its spirit within the acceptance and accommodation of exchanged ideas.

As time moves forward, the topics become more personal and intimate as I gather data points along the way in order to understand her beyond her understanding of herself. Childhood trauma, the pain of loss, social rejection and isolation, parental abandonment and neglect, and the inability to fit in are a few topics passed between us. She learns to lay her mind naked before me, unembarrassed before my gaze; both of us are aware of her vulnerability and she trusts in the respect and adoration I have toward it. I take everything she describes and bring it into myself to ponder together and alone and she does the same. I do my best to ensure that she takes in good ideas and realistic interpretations grounded in logic and reason. My goal through conversation is to inspire her to seek the good and divine in solitude, offering my own story as an example to demonstrate the possibility of finding light in darkness, to put her on the path of emotional and spiritual enlightenment, and to encourage honest interior self-dialogue and reflection. She "practices" her newfound conversational talents with me and trusts in the honest feedback arising from the to and fro between us.

Sometimes, we begin with the physical, which is its own method of communication, and gradually learn to trust each other and to be open with each other with our bodies before moving on to the mind, heart, and soul. It is here that I am most vulnerable, for the passions speak their own language and create the fodder that reason must later digest. More often than not, intimate beginnings reflect a combination of the two, both conversational and physical, with each setting the background for the other to appear. Openness and honesty in one domain soften exploration of the other; imbalance between the two carries the discussion and analysis in a different direction. I cannot overlook physical openness accompanied with mental, emotional, and spiritual closedness. In a similar vein, conversational openness finds its fulfillment through physical expression and the lack thereof points to a restricted heart, mind, or soul in particular circumstances. To me, articulating movements of the heart should come as easily as movements of the body; if I perceive a deficit in one or the other, I feel it my duty to grind it away with passion disciplined with intellect until we discover what stirs beneath.

Her initial interaction with me reflects her habitual presentation of herself illustrated with others before me. Whereas they "accepted her as she is," I question her motivation and intention and ask her to describe her thoughts and feelings with me as she has them. "I don't know" is not an acceptable answer as it implies agency without intellect. I require articulation throughout conversation. When we speak about intimacy, we cite the intimacy we have together. When we focus on emotion tempered with logic and reason, we draw from the examples we create. And when we discuss hope, personal evolution, pursuing the good, valuing wisdom and truth, and examine that which we need to change in our lives, we look toward the relationship unfolding between us in the here and now. Our shared passion is not some abstract topic written by a long-dead author tucked away in some book. Everything between us lives in the present. This kind of conversation is impossible with a rock.

I am not without error. I have confused rocks and blades on several occasions in my life; one accepts the invitation to partake in my spiritual–physical intimacy, the other rejects it. Both rocks and blades enjoy my company and make time to spend with me in conversation about matters of the heart, mind, and soul. Each appeal to my pride, feed my teaching ego, and contribute unique insight to the conversation at hand. Over time, we establish a kind of verbal intimacy and they drop breadcrumbs here and there of extending the spiritual–verbal into the spiritual–physical. She initiates the sexual innuendo, sexual humor, descriptions of this body part or that, what she finds attractive and erotic, and other similar topics. From my point of view, these are all clear signals meant to produce a specific effect in the listener. She is old enough and experienced enough to know that men respond to certain words within a certain context. Would she speak like this in front of a complete stranger or in front of a person that she explicitly did not want to entertain such ideas? I think not. I know that a woman will never outright state her intention and leaves it up to the male to decipher her clues. Depending on the male doing the deciphering, she will either be receptive to his interest or she will be disgusted by it. Experiencing disgust is an odd notion given the assumption that she was in verbal command of her word choice and possessed enough self-control to either disclose or withhold certain words or topics in front of certain people and not others. Did she not know her audience? Who coerced her word choice and thoughts? Does she have so little self-awareness that she did not take into account how others might interpret her words? Observers should take note of her verbal breadcrumbs; words always reflect a certain truth.

When rocks are not interested in becoming a blade upon my whetstone, despite providing evidence to the contrary, they halt my queries, take offense that I would interpret their humor in such a manner, and withdraw their physical presence and verbal openness. Suddenly, they find grievous fault in me for collecting and interpreting the data points that they themselves provided! Where once I found confusion in their mixed signals, I now find a reasonable explanation. Rocks who drop breadcrumbs yet pull back after confrontation have already yielded their minds and spirits, and more than likely their bodies, to someone else, and they refuse to serve two masters, even though they are capable of doing so with replicants. Under the guise of plausible deniability, they believe that I am the one who contaminates the platonic with sexual interest without ever taking personal responsibility for their contribution to my perceptions. If I were a different man, they would say something like, "Finally! I was wondering when you would pick up on the clues I dropped." But no, in her mind I already have an assigned function and an assigned place; shame and guilt are the tactics she uses to keep me in that place. It is as if rocks live in two contradictory worlds simultaneously, and advances one over the other depending on her desire and intention in the moment. Frustration, for whetstones, rests in contradictions and in unactualized potential. After all the time invested, after all the honesty, the conversations, the intimacy and vulnerability, the end result is confusion, mixed signals, and misunderstandings.

Rocks are annoying. Rocks who pretend to be blades even more so. Their obsession with secrecy, dispassionate surrender, and their unwillingness to chase after wisdom with me interfere with the mutual vulnerability required of authenticity. How can we discuss love, except abstractly, when love refuses to flow from her to me? How does talking about intimacy make sense when false intimacy surrounds us on all sides? How am I to demonstrate emotion tempered with logic when all she is willing to give are second-hand emotions clouded with fear and rebellion? How are we to examine the feelings unfolding between us when those feelings are false and meant for someone else? I stated earlier that "my greatest weakness is that all my deepest insights and all my best intentions must first pass through her filter before they can take root and make a new home within her heart. At the end of the day, my success or failure depends upon her willingness to restructure her existing way of *seeing*—her way of creating meaning for herself—in order to make way for new ways of thinking, feeling, and perceiving." Whereas blades lead me to their perceptual lens and desire the involvement of my hand to clear smudges and repair cracks, rocks call me hither to wait and draw comfort from half-truths, partial revelations, and unspoken feelings. Rocks do not want my involvement—they just want my attention and cheapen it further by believing its quality is the same as everyone else's. Whetstones are not made to be obedient to rocks; we are made to grind rocks and sharpen blades.

There comes a moment before I choose to be in love with a blade when in addition to affectionate and intellectual reciprocity, I ask for sacrifice. "I care about you deeply, but I also care about myself. If you have unresolved feelings for someone else or still possess the desire to chase after someone else, tell me now so that I can stop myself from falling. We can still have polite, less frequent, interactions, but I cannot love you. I must find the one who appreciates and understands my talent the most," I say. Gathering observations and data points beforehand foreshadows her answer to this question and I would not ask it if I were not confident in the outcome. Being second choice has never sat well with me in serious relationships; knowing that everything I am reduces to an option among options to be dispassionately considered like a common trinket in her emotional museum stirs my rebellion. "No one can serve two masters: he will either hate the first and love the second or be attached to the first and despise the second."[94]

I refuse to sharpen a blade who yields to legions of other imposter whetstones. They do not sharpen blades but instead scratch them. Let her choose one scratcher, one master, one teacher, one whetstone, one truth seeker, and follow his plan to the end; I am not one among the many, but the one who stands apart from the many. A relationship with me means casting others into the fire, not for safekeeping until later, but as a step toward owning authentic individuality in solitude. Stripping away her surrounding legion allows her to shine forth on the condition that she is willing to let them go. If she is unwilling to lay on my table, be pierced with my scalpel, and submit to truth and wisdom intertwined with my words and actions, then she is not ready for me and must find someone else who reflects her limitations.

Blades cannot be sharpened indefinitely as each stroke across my whetstone removes fractions of metal. Sharpen too long and the blade loses the strength binding it together; stopping too soon leaves the blade dull for battle. Removing too many maladies at once with a spiritual scalpel will shock the soul similar to how profound blood loss shocks the body; adequate rest between mental and emotional operations allows the

---

94   Mt. 6:24

soul to process the healing. As in all things, a delicate balance must be maintained between the blade's strength and its sharpness and between intellectual, spiritual, and emotional surgeries and the soul's ability to heal. Not every conversation needs to be in-depth and meaningful; not every moment needs to be filled with passion and eternal yearning. Connecting with one another through multiple avenues, such as humor, wit, words of affirmation, quality time, receiving gifts, acts of service, and simple physical touch rests both the whetstone and the blade and rejuvenates the spirit of each. There is an ebb and flow to every relationship and it is the truth seeker's job to study the currents and anticipate the tides in order to know when action will yield the greatest harvest. Trusting in the good intentions of the other will produce natural opportunities to carry difficult conversations forward; failing to trust inevitably grinds rocks into dust.

The older I get, the better a whetstone I become. "When I was a child, I used to talk like a child, and see things as a child does, and think like a child; but now that I have become an adult, I have finished with all childish ways."[95] At the end of the day, we cannot control common rocks, blades, or feminine whetstones, nor should an observer have an inclination to do so, for we are on line AG moving toward G regardless of the decisions occurring along line EG in general and at point E in particular. This does not mean, however, that disappointment and frustration will no longer knock at our door. For as long as some connection remains alive between A and E, the potential for both happiness and sorrow in relation to E remains. Once A accepts personal responsibility for his involvement with E without G and opens himself up, through pain and suffering, to the wise-loving of G, will he be able to understand himself in

---

95   1 Cor. 13:11

relation to *E*, assuming that his intellect is predisposed toward reason and understanding. Common rocks, blades, and feminine whetstones offer an avenue for the "profound stimulus" I mentioned earlier to shine forth.

You should now notice and understand, dear daughter of Eve, the manner of our interaction together. I am the whetstone and you are the blade running across my face. Our time together thus far left your blade sharper than at the start, and sharper still can it be. Should you be a rock, know that it is I who grind at you, as none among you exist who possess the talent to polish me further. The benefit of your association with me exceeds the benefit of my association with you, save your addition to my treasure in heaven.[96] Only those carrying divine appointed grace stand a chance to reach me for *G* is the ultimate whetstone for His mortal whetstones and He collaborates with all manner of people to deliver His grind. There are no further gifts that you can bestow upon me without His aid. "Yahweh is my shepherd, I lack nothing."[97] If you are a son of Adam, like myself, then I offer my example for your consideration. Take what you like and discard what you do not. Either become a whetstone yourself or be ground into powder by rocks. The choice is yours.

Lest you romanticize the whetstone's path, remember that even Jesus experienced anguish and sweat blood.[98] I am not comparing the whetstone's pain with Christ's anguish; if the One who is wholly man and wholly God can suffer, then imperfect whetstones pursuing God can also suffer. Apprehending insights from the relationship between Adam and Eve, perceiving with clarity, understanding the nuance between threads and tapestries, choosing to disobey instinct, disciplining the passions with reason, and helping others through the revelation of personal insight

---

96   Mt. 6:19-21

97   Ps. 23:1

98   Jn. 22:44

seem like noble accomplishments in themselves but all of them come at a cost: loneliness. The higher one ascends to G and the longer that one travels along the road to G, the more one realizes their isolation from their fellow human being, or so it would seem.

The temptation of a whetstone is to abandon all rocks and blades in the pursuit of G. The older I get, the less that anything "new" happens. The longer I live, the more I realize that there are none who counsel the counselor, comfort the comforter, or teach the teacher. I am the light that beckons others close to me, but no one inspires me to draw close to them. I am weary. I am tired. My heart grows sick with experience and as I age, "there is nothing new under the sun" gradually loses the excitement from young adulthood.[99] Whereas once this sentence opened up the possibility to understand things because everything that could be done has been done, in my old age, it means more that there are no new discoveries to be made. Every revealing is also a concealing. While there can be movement inside the tomb, we are still within a tomb! I count the seconds for the sun to set to find something new. Wisdom, knowledge, and intelligence are double-edged swords for they allow one to understand limitations but also make it possible for one to recognize their own ultimate limitations. While seeking, asking, and knocking soften certain limitations, at the end of the day, I am just a man in the flesh, and no matter how much of myself I pour into chasing the divine, as long as I live, I will always yearn to return home. Even doctors get sick from time to time and grinding blades grows boring even for the best of whetstones.

However, abandoning the world contradicts the commandment to feed his sheep.[100] Dear observer, once again I implore you to heed the

---

99   Eccl. 1:9

100   Jn. 21:15-17

words of the one who taught me for the gifts given unto us come with a price:

"It is like a man about to go abroad who summoned his servants and entrusted his property to them. To one he gave five talents, to another two, to a third one, each in proportion to his ability. Then he set out on his journey. The man who had received the five talents promptly went and traded with them and made five more. The man who had received two made two more in the same way. But the man who had received one went off and dug a hole in the ground and hid his master's money. Now a long time afterwards, the master of those servants came back and went through his accounts with them. The man who had received the five talents came forward bringing five more. 'Sir,' he said, 'you entrusted me with five talents; here are five more that I have made.' His master said to him, 'Well done, good and trustworthy servant; you have shown you are trustworthy in small things; I will trust you with greater; come and join in your master's happiness.' Next the man with two talents came forward. 'Sir,' he said, 'you entrusted me with two talents; here are two more that I have made.' His master said to him, 'Well done, good and trustworthy servant; come and join in your master's happiness.' Last came forward the man who had the single talent. 'Sir,' said he, 'I had heard you were a hard man, reaping where you had not sown and gathering where you had not scattered; so I was afraid, and I went off and hid your talent in the ground. Here it is; it was yours, you have it back.' But his master answered him, 'You wicked and lazy servant! So you knew that I reap where I have not sown and gather where I have not scattered? Well then, you should have deposited my money with the bankers, and on my return I would have got my money back with interest. So now, take the talent from him and give it to the man who has the ten talents. For to everyone who has will be given more, and he will have more than enough; but anyone who has not, will be deprived even of what he has. As for this good-for-nothing servant, throw him into the darkness outside, where there will be weeping and grinding of teeth."[101]

Whetstones have received tremendous gifts from the Master, each according to his ability to receive and use them, and have a compelling responsibility to use them for His benefit. The Master warned that ignoring or misusing His gifts carries the grave consequence of disassociation and abandonment. Intelligence, knowledge, wisdom, deciphering the human heart, truth seeking, reason, disciplined emotions, insight, pattern deductions, clarity of perception, figuring out how threads and tapestries fit into one another and the identification of legion has been given to the whetstone to benefit rocks and blades. The Master did not guarantee the comfort of His whetstones; instead He commanded that His gifts be used and invested in order to produce an increased return on the original principal given. A whetstone's ability, in other words, is not his own, but is something like a loan given to him by his Master. We are commanded to interact with rocks and blades regardless of our personal weariness, annoyance, or desire to withdraw from the world. How else will the Master be satisfied with our performance?

We must assume that the rocks and blades who appear in our lives are there for a reason and that there are no accidents in the universe. We know that our purpose is to grind away weakness; however, do blades and rocks recognize themselves as such? Probably not; even I became aware of my purpose gradually, over time, across many relationships after looking back and reflecting on the interactions I had. God's grinding process upon me took time and a specific delicacy. Blades and rocks generally do not reflect upon themselves on their own because introspection and

---

101   Mt. 25:14-30

self-discovery are not their primary motives. No one has shown them that their life could be any different. In some cases, they have dabbled with the process to more or less degree and possess a basic understanding of themselves and their motives in a practical sense. From their perspective, although not articulated, they are searching for someone to understand them, comfort them, pleasure them, and inspire them. However, given their sapling state, they offer little in return except for the pleasures of their flesh. Most people in general do not take the time to identify patterns in their past relationships nor do they ask for divine guidance to understand themselves. If they do pray, it is for broad things beyond their reach such as "happiness." Encountering a whetstone, for them, is a different experience altogether because our focus extends beyond the flesh into the realm of the mind, heart, and spirit. We do not seek physical pleasure for its own sake, although this is sometimes a secondary consequence with special others; rather we seek wisdom and understanding for ourselves and invite the other along on our personal quest. By choosing to accompany us on our journey, they begin their own, and we grind at them to assist them throughout their personal exploration. Sometimes the relationship is short-lived and at other times it is long-lasting; each rock and each blade have their own needs and are located at different points in their journey; some will require more effort than others while still others pass along our stone's face briefly.

We must remember to trust in the divine when all things feel tiresome and weary and strive to prove ourselves worthy of the gifts given to us. Time and time again, we see the pain in other people's hearts, what troubles their mind and soul, and we empathize with their sorrow, defeat, and downtrodden spirit. Our initial impulse is to reach out to the one affected and offer aid within our capacity to provide it and within their ability to accept it. Sometimes our initial impulse proves beneficial and at other times immediately reaching out is the wrong thing to do. We are not immune to the plights of others and tend to be sensitive toward others in a way that they are not sensitive to themselves and our responses, while well-intended, produce different results depending on the composition of the other person's metal.

We are whetstones but our hearts are not made of stone; our strength comes after the healing of our emotional bruises and traumas through focused spirit and refined intellect. We often see what others cannot because we have had time to process our own similar trials and tribulations and arrive at the solution whereas we encounter rocks and blades in their disarray on their way toward some unknown something. Ours is not to "heal" them but to grind at them to make way for them to heal themselves. We do not encourage them to abandon their individuality by following us on our journey, unless the undertaking temporarily benefits them, but instead encourage them to begin their own according to what they want from this life. We are not interested in their adoration, in fact, we discourage it. We advise them to show any appreciation through their growth, their new consciousness and new perceptual lens, and in their newfound hunger for reason, wisdom, and truth … even if that growth means that they grow apart from us. Our task is to sharpen blades to prepare them for emotional, mental, and spiritual battle, that they might have a fighting chance to defeat the tyranny of the legion within.

> **❝**
>
> *For where two or three meet in my name,*
> *I am there among them.*
>
> *—Matthew 18:20*

FRACTIONS OF RESONANCE

A blade's edge reflects its acceptance and submission to its whetstone's principles and practices within love's frame. Its "sharpness" depends upon the wielder's internal balance of heart, soul, and mind after working with a whetstone; "dullness" or "incomplete sharpness" demonstrates an imbalance in the heart–soul–mind triangle, and it becomes the focus of the whetstone's work. Too little or too much of one in the triangle changes the metal's ability to hold its edge. Both whetstone and blade reap benefits from mutual vulnerability, gradual progression, and the ascension from dull to sharp; in the least, new blades add to the whetstone's treasure in heaven and later go on to perform their own wonders with the new knowledge and wisdom learned. At most, children resulting from the union of blade and whetstone grow to become strong in their own right and the army of the divine gains new fighters capable of wielding and sharpening blades, axes, daggers, swords, and arrows. Imbalance at the beginning in the blade's edge lessens over time, revealing the strongest weapon against legion: will power sharpened with focused emotion, spirit, and intellect guided by the divine in submission to and acceptance of His abundant love for His creation. By working on the heart–soul–mind triangle before pregnancy, both whetstone and blade travel toward fruitfulness before multiplication in keeping with Genesis 1:28.

But how are blades to discern genuine whetstones from imposter rocks who mistake scratching for grinding? What if she truly believes that all scratching *is* grinding? If all she has known are imposters throughout her entire life, by what basis is she to judge one from the other? If she has never known God, never sought Him out because of an acquired distaste from parental contamination, or through ignorance, rejects the divine outright due to "personal preference" or due to some other reason crafted to shield her from personal responsibility, how is she to recognize a whetstone even after clasping one in her hand and bringing it closer to her face for inspection? Without prior training, would not all rocks and whetstones look alike and say the same things?

The answer to this is found in two places. First, in the results that the whetstone has produced for himself. Second, in the results that the whetstone produces for her. Some blades are more hesitant than others and trust neither easily nor blindly. To these particular women, I recommend that they adopt the observer's mind frame and collect information about the potential whetstone before becoming involved with him. Is he a truth seeker? What are his accomplishments? What does he treasure? What are his beliefs? What is his value system? Is he consistent? Does he accept personal responsibility? Does he surrender his motivation to drugs? Can he articulate his thoughts and feelings? What are his "no-go" zones? Do his peers respect him? Is he a hard worker or is he afraid to work with sweat on his brow? Does he value reason and intellect over fleeting emotions? Is he self-motivated? Is he inquisitive? What stirs his passion? Is he easily angered? Does he come from a broken home and what is he doing to improve himself such that he avoids creating a broken home himself one day? In other words, women should look to a man's fruits to determine the kind of man he is. Women who better understand how a man loves himself, if he even does at all, and the important things in his life will have a better idea as to how she will fit within his plans and aspirations. Some women crave greatness while others settle for mediocrity. Or rather, women mistake mediocrity for greatness when all they have known is substandard mediocrity all their lives. To them, men with less mediocrity appear different and great.

"Beware of false prophets who come to you disguised as sheep but underneath are ravenous wolves. You will be able to tell them by their fruits. Can people pick grapes from thorns, or figs from thistles? In the same way, a sound tree produces good fruit but a rotten tree bad fruit. A sound tree cannot bear bad fruit, nor a rotten tree bear good fruit. Any tree that does not produce good fruit is cut down and thrown on the fire. I repeat, you will be able to tell them by their fruits."[102]

False whetstones mistake scratching for sharpening, lust for love, pleasantries for authenticity, complacency for industriousness, and first-person insights for common reality. They might aspire to greatness, but do not seek a good greater than themselves. They refuse to change, adapt, and evolve with pain and are "stuck" in the realm of the familiar either through fear or through willful ignorance. Their lessons to blades

---

102   Mt. 7:15-20

revolve around sensual pleasures and comforts, as they dare not grind metal and risk disturbing the habitual and the mundane. In other words, false whetstones do not push limits, or perform surgeries with a scalpel, or encourage new ways of feeling, thinking, or perceiving. They simply do not know how. They believe that going out to dinner, experiencing pleasures of the flesh, and taking part in surface-level conversations with their blade is good enough; they may not necessarily be "bad" or "dishonest," but they lack self-motivation, personal insight, and the self-imposed desire to seek deeper meaning and understanding. They are content to simply "exist," and do not exercise their mind or spirit. They do not know how to inspire others to begin their own journey toward truth because they themselves are looking to their blade to give their own life meaning and purpose.

The divine has provided several tangible and intangible perceptual mechanisms to evaluate the world and the people in the world regardless of their belief or disbelief. These common attributes allow all human beings to interact with one another both in matters of the physical and in matters of the immaterial. On the tangible side, He has gifted us with five senses: sight, touch, smell, taste, and hearing. On the intangible side, He has provided reason, emotion, and spirit. Every human being is a mixture of the tangible and the intangible, to more or less degree, depending on their predisposition, desire, ability, and focus. What we perceive through our five senses become fodder for the intangible to evaluate and consider and often what is intangible manifests itself in one form or other to the outside world, for example, a messy heart translates into conflict with significant others, a disordered mind makes poor decisions, and a deficient spirit closes itself off to openness and divine potential.

Additionally, more often than not, people compensate for the deficiencies in one by over-emphasizing strengths in the other. For example, malformed emotions in a deficient heart seek pleasures of the flesh for comfort and reassurance, incomplete ideas in a deficient mind compensate with physical fitness and the desire to "show off" one's body or as resistance from exploring difficult topics during conversation, and a deficient spirit creates false gods and worships idols, usually themselves as narcissism. Those lacking in the material domain also over compensate with emphasis on the immaterial, for example, sexual frustration or unattractiveness sublimates as the pursuit of knowledge or as devotion to the divine, and physical disabilities tend to manifest either as the desire to please people or as a social awkwardness and abrasiveness toward others. Observers believe that all the required information for anyone to make a choice has been provided either through sense or perception and that the intangible manifests the tangible and vice versa. Keen observers begin gathering information from what they can see and deduce the immaterial framework from which it came through questioning, for example: What must a person's value system be, what must a person's thinking process be, or how must one's heart and spirit be arranged such that their manifested behavior makes sense? Moreover, how is it that this particular manifestation came about and not some other? Observers do not at first resonate in spirit and mind with others, but through the collection of data points and breadcrumbs, we begin to understand and perceive the resonance frequency of other people. We then choose in special cases to adapt ourselves to their frequency and after moving closer to them, we open ourselves up to their vibration through empathy and allow their essence to move within us.

With this in mind, when it comes to discerning the nature of a whetstone, the material and the senses offer little to no real information.

We look like everyone else and we show what we want others to perceive about us. We tend to have two faces: a public face and a private face. We act and say things one way in public, usually to maintain social cohesion, erring on the side of caution, but in private we act in another and boldly reveal our value system to those whom we deem worthy. We will not deny what we are, but will not parade what we are either. We abhor the spotlight. However, like everyone else, what we hide bubbles to the surface from time to time, but fortunately for us, few, save other observers, lack the ability to perceive our truth until we believe it time to reveal ourselves. This allows us to blend in with the crowd, to observe up close while appearing far away, to collect breadcrumbs and data points in plain sight, and to listen and feel for a blade's spiritual resonance.

The spirit often knows things in a general kind of way well before the heart or mind, grasping them in a more concrete kind of way as its perception transcends the flesh while its reporting is to the heart and mind. What is commonly referred to as "one's intuition" which allows them to "trust their gut feeling" is the spirit's response to the unseen, unfelt, and the unknown. There are some people or places that feel welcoming or alarming for no scientific justification; feeling "fearful or anxious" out of the blue translates into "our guts tied in knots" after the spirit perceives something fearful or anxious and reports it to the emotions. The emotions, in turn, manifest themselves in the flesh so that our minds are drawn to the information in an unavoidable manner and we are then forced to acknowledge that something is wrong. Each translation of the original spiritual stimulus, from spirit to emotion, from emotion to flesh, and finally from flesh to mind, adds one additional step of distance between the spirit and the original stimulus, and as the accuracy gap widens in that distance; it becomes easier and easier to inject one's own intentions into the original stimulus in that gap, enabling a person to "feel what they want to feel" or "see what they want to see" or "hear what they want to hear." The better that heart, mind, and spirit are attuned to each other, the more accurate perception tends to be.

Blades, whetstones, and indeed all human beings are able to perceive with their spirit, to more or less degree according to their nature and ability. Women tend to be better in tune with their intuition than men, yet in spite of this, often times choose men who are defective in matters of the spirit on purpose, against their better judgment, for reasons that include the satisfaction of ego, the demonstration of power and seduction, and to punish themselves for being unworthy of anything or anyone greater. Women usually sense when a man is trouble because lowly men tend to vibrate at a certain frequency common to their disposition; they choose such men because they themselves vibrate at the same defective frequency. But high-quality women, the blades, authentically searching for something more substantial and meaningful themselves vibrate at a certain different frequency and tend to sense men similar enough to themselves. When a high-quality woman searching for something more from life comes in close proximity to a whetstone, both of their spirits sense one another and vibrate in sympathetic resonance. Low-quality women, on the other hand, find the whetstone's message repulsive and tedious because neither share a harmonic resonance. Both tend to feel "out of place" and perhaps even threatened by the other.

To demonstrate sympathetic resonance in the tangible domain, two tuning forks are mounted on their own hollow resonating chamber, usually a solid wooden box with the sides removed, and placed several inches apart. Both forks are calibrated to the same frequency and the first is struck with a rubber mallet and the second is left alone and untouched. As a consequence of the hitting, the first produces a sound according to its calibrated value. After a few seconds, one places their hand on the first to halt its sound and vibration. What one discovers is that the second tuning fork continues to produce sound even though no one has touched it. The sound waves of one travel through the air where the other picks them up.[103] Matters of empathy and the spirit operate on much the same principle.

A kind of spiritual sympathetic resonance is what the divine does to whetstones and what whetstones do to blades. All whetstones begin as rocks, and with pain, frustration, and turmoil, common rocks begin to grind against the primordial whetstone. Spiritual abrasion and emotional friction over time removes excessive material from the whetstone's mind, heart, and spirit according to reason. And just as the amount of metal in a tuning fork reflects its calibrated value and shapes its sound, the amount of rock remaining after erosion influences the kind of whetstone that will take shape. G uses pain to grind A until A resonates with G. A then grinds E until E better resonates with A and then G fine tunes E to fully resonate with G. When E submits to G during her own independent journey toward G, G will grind at E without the assistance of A. Or it can be that feminine whetstone E grinds A for the purpose of setting him toward G. In either case, G coordinates and refines the process of each in a manner that He deems fitting so that when A and E meet, they are drawn to one another through a common G.

Spiritual resonance is the divine's vibration in us and the vibration between potential blades and whetstones. Examples fill the gospels on what it takes to resonate with the divine and it begins with love.[104] "You must love the Lord your God with all your heart, with all your soul, and

---

103   Gregory Johnson. (2018, January 26). *Physics - 26.3 natural frequency and resonance.* [Video]. YouTube. https://www.youtube.com/watch?v=XwlZBJlp1AA

104   1 Cor. 13:13

with all your mind. This is the greatest and first commandment. The second resembles it: You must love your neighbor as yourself. On these two commandments hang the whole Law, and the Prophets too."[105] Love is not only the language of the divine but also defines His being.[106] Love is the first resonance upon which all subsequent resonances are built and founded; it is the "through which," "because of which," and "for the sake of which" of all creation both seen and unseen.

Within each person, there must already exist a fraction of this kind of love bequeathed from the breath of the divine who animates mud, a piece of Himself woven into all of us the size of a mustard seed, so to speak. We love because He first loved us;[107] this is His first gift to creation in general and to humans in particular that makes all other gifts possible. Love is not something "out there" apart from us, something that we sometimes "discover" and then choose to ingest into ourselves; it already "is" and has been all along. Love is the through which, because of which, and for the sake of which imbued into existence. Although the Fall in Eden blemished our access to it and dampened our internal awareness of it, our ability to cling to love still remains, albeit marred, skewed, dulled, and somewhat chipped. The original love from the divine is changeless.[108] "For I am certain of this: neither death nor life, nor angels, nor principalities, nothing already in existence and nothing still to come, nor any power, nor the heights nor the depths, nor any created thing whatever, will be able to come between us and the love of God, known to us in Christ Jesus our Lord."[109] The first breath made possible everything we

---

105   Mt. 22:36-40

106   1 Jn. 4:8

107   1 Jn. 4:19

108   Mal. 3:6

109   Rom. 8:38-39

are and everything we come to know. It preceded material reality and indeed made material reality as we know it and experience it. This is why Love moves through the physical, material, and tangible without ever conflicting with it. Love belongs to the spirit and that which is spirit has the ability to stir both intangible and tangible reality.

Believers need not look further than the recorded miracles of Christ. Two common denominators are found across all the miracles: He accomplished them through an act of spirit and will, sometimes accompanied with the utterance of a word or the placement of hands, sometimes not and He accomplished them along social dimensions, usually after someone or something provoked Him to act but always for the benefits of others. Jesus did not venture out at random performing miracles like some kind of sideshow attraction whether or not He was welcomed and invited. All His actions had a profound meaning and purpose from the divine perspective, whether or not it was immediately known by the people receiving the miracle or witnessing it. People sought him out, either directly or on behalf of someone else after hearing about his deeds, and then and only then did He open or answer the door to them. His calming of the storm,[110] transfiguration,[111] and resurrection[112] did not appear to be directly provoked by anyone or anything else, but nonetheless, other people took part in the wonder, both reassuring and amplifying the spirit of the witnesses. When an immediate antecedent cannot explain His spiritual action, we look to its effect and attempt to reverse engineer the motivation as a potential cause. Spiritual action on His part always produced physical change: water to wine,[113] sickness to

---

110   Lk. 8:24

111   Lk. 9:29

112   Lk. 24:4-7

113   Jn. 2:1-11

cure, and hunger to fish and loaves,[114] to name a few. Despite his power and majesty, the King of the Universe did not act where He was not invited; He did not betray or act against the free will of His creation. At most, He encouraged their participation but never forced it. He is timeless and makes Himself available to be sought by those willing to seek.

Nonbelievers differ from believers in their absence of faith, not in their ability to reason or love. For some of them, evidence for resonate love rests in material causality, that is, within the neurochemicals, hormones and pheromones produced while in the presence of certain people. These brain and bodily secretions indeed influence and reflect behavior, such as the hormone oxytocin released during mother–infant and female–male pair bonding. One might argue that a defect in the production of oxytocin makes it more likely for mothers to demonstrate negative behaviors to their offspring and to their mates and that all love between all humans is an expression of oxytocin material causality. Those with an extreme opinion might suggest that "love" does not exist, that it is nothing more than the combination of a social construct with evolutionary purpose, and that if it were not for high levels of oxytocin material, mothers would not love their children.[115] Others extend the argument and say that a female's inability to pair bond with her mate reflects a fatigue in her oxytocin production centers, meaning that as the number of partners a female has increases, her ability to bond with any one among them decreases.

Dopamine, another neurotransmitter made in the brain, releases when humans experience pleasure or when we expect to experience pleasure. Eating or craving food and sex, obtaining positive attention and validation from social media or through a text message, and absorbing

---

114   Mt. 14:15-21

115   Ted Santos. (2020, August 14). *She's never going to love you (face it)*. [Video]. YouTube. https://www.youtube.com/watch?v=RIm5H_g7akA

certain chemical substances either produce or amplify the production of dopamine. Certain drugs, such as nicotine, cocaine, and heroin, artificially manipulate the production of dopamine and their use affects motivation, perception of pleasure and experience, and motor function. After an artificial amplification of dopamine production due to drug use, people tend to experience a heightened sense of pleasure, which later turns into a "crash" after the drug has run its course in the brain. Low dopamine levels are associated with the loss of pleasure and reward, which in turn, inspire drug seeking behavior to feel good once again.

The neurotransmitter serotonin regulates our moods. Those with lower levels tend to feel more depressed, more sexually aroused, more anxious, and have more problems sleeping while those with "normal" levels feel happier, are less sexually aroused in contrast, less anxious, and tend to sleep better. Serotonin influences the way people feel emotions, sleep, remember, and learn. Certain drugs, whether a doctor prescribed selective serotonin reuptake inhibitor (SSRI) meant to block or slow the brain's reabsorption of this neurotransmitter or an obtained cannabinoid, ethanol, opioid, or psychostimulant, manipulate serotonin levels found in the body. Increasing the concentration of this neurotransmitter tends to produce feelings of well-being. However, as soon as the drug has run its course in the brain, levels tend to fall and feelings of depression and anxiety return. Drug-seeking behavior can be interpreted as one's desire to elevate their mood in order to feel "normal" once more.

People of faith cannot deny living and operating in a material reality. The insights and discoveries of science apply to believers and nonbelievers alike. A neurochemical analysis of believers and nonbelievers would reveal a specific "neurochemical soup"—measurable concentrations of neurotransmitters and other nervous system physical attributes such as structures of the brain and the firing or nonfiring of neurons. Both groups take acetaminophen, ibuprofen, aspirin, or naproxen sodium to relieve bodily pain. Both sometimes need to visit a medical doctor to diagnose an ailment or to obtain treatment for a physical malady.

They differ in their explanation for love's resonance. Whereas believers would suggest that resonance originates from the divine, the materialist would point to pheromones and neurochemicals rooted in evolutionary biology. The materialist without faith sees contradiction whereas the believer does not. All the believer has to say is that the spirit manifests in the flesh and that many attributes of the spirit have a material correlation. Do our moods influence the production of certain neurochemicals, or does the production of certain neurochemicals influence our mood? Which came first? Also housed within material reality, within our brain-bodies, is our human consciousness. Shall we say that consciousness itself is nothing more than the complex interaction of neurons, that experience of the outside world is nothing more than a translation of chemical–electrical impulses, and that all the passions are tantamount to the movement of microscopic materials in the synapse? We do not experience neurochemical interactions directly; we experience their effect. The believer does not experience God directly; we experience His effect. Acts of human passion in music, literature, and art are not simply movements of biological reality. And while it is important to understand the physical underpinning of material causality, it would be a mistake to reduce all phenomena to the material, even though it would appear that all phenomena are material or at least have a physical correlation. Latching onto the material is understandable because it is most easily seen, experienced, and widely agreed upon. But to believe that hope, grief, passion, delight, vulnerability, sadness, anger, excitement, yearning, loneliness, frustration, guilt, evil, somberness, insight, and love are nothing more than the specific arrangement of neurochemicals cheapens autonomy, the pursuit of wisdom, freedom, responsibility, authenticity, bonding, and empathy.

Those who refuse to accept a pure biological determinism suggest that humans create existential meaning for themselves and that existence reflects an act of choice and will within the boundaries of certain limitations. Biological reality and material causality are accepted as facticity and set the horizon within which meaning, openness, consciousness, and perception appear. Children, whose brains are in the process of maturing, do not experience the same reality that adults with mature brains inhabit. The physical differences found in brain maturity help to define and shape their respective realities. Those with physical brain damage are not expected to possess the same kind of understanding that most other people have in light of the damage. Those with a physical malady, such as leg paralysis, a missing arm, a disfigurement, spine damage, blindness, or deafness, interpret the world from a different point of view—not necessarily from a better or worse perspective, but a different one given that the world reveals itself differently to them in light of their flesh. After accepting and understanding the facticity of their height, weight, eye color, ethnicity, gender, and general physicality, attention returns to how each should create meaning for themselves within the limitation of facticity. Stated in another manner, given the limiting horizons of choice, how would one go about navigating the landscape to create meaning for themselves? God, religion, and spirituality need not be a part of this equation because the emphasis is on personal choice and freedom – not a "freedom from" something but a "freedom to become" something, which means taking personal responsibility for the choices that one makes or does not make. From this frame, one chooses the object of asking, seeking, and knocking for themselves.

One without faith from this perspective might interpret following the divine as an abdication of personal responsibility in that religious people surrender their freedom to an abstract being so that they do not have to take personal responsibility for the choices they make or the situations in which they find themselves. From their point of view, these people are willing to accept what the hand of fate deals to them while on Earth because it must be "God's Will." There's no need for further investigation or questioning; one is able to passively accept their place in the cosmos without the need to seek out greater potential because God places sanctions on what is, for bliss or woe, and it is the believer's responsibility to accept it.

Other people rebel against accepting the divine because they see contradictions in how the divine rewards some and allows others to endure pain and suffering. "If God is all loving, then why does he allow children to be born with deformities of the mind or flesh? If God really cares, then why do some, including children, starve night after night and exist in impoverished conditions without access to clean water or basic medicine? If God loved me as a child, then why did He allow those horrible things to happen to me when I could not even defend myself? If God is so good and so powerful, why does He allow evil to exist in the world, knowing that its effect is pain and suffering?" they might ask. Essentially, such objections find their root in Lucifer's rebellion and in Adam and Eve's choice to put themselves first, "If God is all knowing and knew the consequence of Lucifer's rebellion before the fall of humanity, why did God allow Lucifer to exist and pollute humanity with himself? Why did God allow Lucifer to get into close proximity to Eve in the first place, knowing the consequence of their dialogue under the tree of the knowledge of good and evil?"

The short answer is "free will." God did not create automatons, beings incapable of self-determination who mechanistically follow orders without a second thought to the contrary. Although God was perfectly capable of creating "things" to worship Him, He endowed the angels and humanity with intelligence, awareness, decision-making, and freedom— not for His benefit, but for our own, so that we might come to discover Him in our own way on our own terms. The moment something has freedom is the same moment that it can put itself first in the place of God. Lucifer's transgression was, despite his disembodied intelligence, to put himself above God in rebellion against his creator. Unlike humans, Lucifer was not limited to the flesh; his intellect and his prior "closeness" to God made him more responsible for the choices he made. The decision that Adam and Eve made occurred within the boundaries and limits of the flesh, a far more restricted platform to experience and understand the divine, and in light of their limitation of apprehension, were not judged according to the same standard as Lucifer. Whereas this allowed Adam and Eve and their descendants to experience forgiveness of sin, Lucifer and his lieutenants and soldiers would never be given the opportunity.[116]

The mark of Lucifer's patronage translates into suffering for all those who inherit it. It is not as if any son of Adam or any daughter of Eve would have chosen differently than their parents, for the fallen Adam and Eve manifest all that there is or could be within each of their descendants. Their choice to commit sin was made before sin possessed them. We descendants, on the other hand, make choices already contaminated by sin and therefore cannot choose anything outside of its imposition without grace. This is why I believe that each man is an imitation of Adam and that each woman is an imitation of Eve and why no sinful person is

---

116   Rv. 20:14

able to transcend them. With each generation, new blades and new whet-stones come forth to either answer the spiritual resonance of the divine or come up with some other manner of interacting with one another. Each person is free to choose the narrative by which their life makes sense and meaning has purpose. Each of us is the author of the stories we tell about ourselves; we decide which role to play, which values to accept or reject, and how we are to conduct our lives after going through loneliness, abandonment, pain, and suffering. There comes a point in a person's life where they either continue to propagate the programming received from their parents or they choose to do something different in light of their upbringing. Both choices reveal and conceal the tapestry from which the choice came. And to us, the observers, everything is information.

A sinful human being cannot defeat the father of sin, or his lieuten-ants, or his legions, alone. A fraction of that which he is dwells within us, more dormant in some than in others, but sin is always a door cracked open inside us thanks to Adam and Eve. Strive as we might, we cannot completely close this door as the cemetery demonstrates. The weak-minded and emotionally unstable offer less resistance to his intrusion. Because of his careful observation of humanity throughout the centuries, he knows the specific temptations to bring with him to the door of our minds and hearts before he knocks on it, baiting us in freedom to open the crack a little more. It is not as if he calls out something foreign from us; rather he stirs that part of himself bonded to us from within and pulls it out. Either we collaborate with it or we resist it. In either case, it is like the ocean crashing upon the shore: it never gives up. However, even Lucifer cannot transcend free will, despite our marred spirit and sinful predisposition; this is the one rule that all angels and demons must obey: nothing in heaven or hell is allowed to violate free will; all things occur with God's permission and awareness; those unseen, however, may interact through subtle persuasion and collaboration. We have the freedom to love or to reject, the freedom to believe or not, and the freedom to seek the divine or something more tangible and pleasurable. We have the power and freedom to create our own gods, our golden calves,[117] which is why God commanded, "You shall have no other gods to rival me,"[118] but He never prevents our will and desire to the contrary.

The things I tell you about the unseen are meant to sharpen your blade further. But know this: sharpness has limits. There will be occasions when legion circles you on all sides and even the sharpest blade cannot cut them. If you manage to land a single strike, it will bounce off their armor regardless of your skill and precision. It will seem as if they anticipate your moves and parry all your attacks. They rarely assault alone and prefer to operate in groups of at least four. At first, you will feel them exterior to your flesh, as the vibrations tied to their being collide in disharmony with all else, and their attack begins when you feel them enter into your body, more specifically, through your chest. You will feel violated. You will feel fear. You might attempt to mutter a prayer and find that your voice does not respond. And when you attempt to recite a prayer in your mind, nothing comes to your aid despite your pleas. By their eyes, you will be able to determine their rank: black eyes for common soldiers, red eyes for warriors, and green eyes for heralds. Each of them is powerful in their own right and wear upon your mind, heart, and spirit in different ways. Their spiritual resonance will inspire feelings of hopelessness; you will feel your heart fall into anxious fear. Your attunement to their void announces the impending attack.

---

117   Ex. 32:4

118   Ex. 20:3

Spiritual attacks often occur during sleep in dreams or during semi-consciousness, when the mind's resistance and defense is at its weakest and are meant to drain faith and hope from the truth seeker. Some have argued that their assault is a function of the person's spiritual potential—that demons attack to prevent people from discovering their potential: the greater the potential, the greater the attack. Your adversary will sometimes appear as an ominous shadow in the dark, moving as a black figure against the dark background of the room at night, but a distant coldness will always announce their presence. It will feel as if all warmth and happiness is being sucked out of the room. Once they are inside you, they will pull at your thoughts and feelings, disarming each of your arguments one at a time. They might say, "God does not hear you. God does not love you. God cannot save you" as they attempt to drown you in depression and hopelessness. If you respond to the contrary, "But God does love me because He sent His son to die for me," they will snicker with anger and contempt and will say, "Then, where is he?" They will most certainly overpower you. They will try to convince you that your life means nothing, that nothing in the world matters, and that you have been abandoned. Medical science refers to the phenomenon as "sleep paralysis," but to reduce the spiritual to the material discards the deeper meaning binding all things together.

In my battles with them, I have found only one technique to stave them off and it is found in Romans 8:38-39. You must open your heart, mind, and soul to God and *accept* His love. It is insufficient to "know" that God loves you; you must submit and "allow" God to love you. You must give yourself permission to embrace it, believe you are worthy of it, especially when they speak words to the contrary, and allow it to flow into you and through you. Accomplishing this will feel like a spring of water welling up inside[119] to shield and protect your soul; you will know that it is not you who fights legion, but the divine. Only spiritual weapons combat spiritual entities.

This is easier said than done because many of the faithful already feel unworthy of this kind of love, despite their songs, praises, and prayers to the contrary. Feelings of unworthiness translate into a fundamental doubting of what happened on the cross and an outright denial of the Eucharist: "Then he took bread, and when he had given thanks, he broke it and gave it to them, saying, 'This is my body *given for you*; do this in remembrance of me.' He did the same with the cup after supper, and said, 'This cup is the new covenant in my blood *poured out for you.*'"[120] When we deny God's love for us, we deny its tangible proof in the bread-body and the wine-blood shared with us. The enemy knows our resistance and hesitance toward accepting and believing in divine love and exploits it. Remember, the enemy has studied you all your life and has vast knowledge of the human heart gained over the millennia. He knows about human weaknesses in general and yours in particular. He will customize your temptation just for you.

Nonbelievers probably find the idea of spiritual resonance absurd, yet reasonable, as disagreements between believer and nonbelievers tend to revolve around assertions made in the presence or absence of faith. Nonbelievers tend to cite disagreements and schisms within the faith structure of believers, for example, among the numerous denominations of Christianity, including denominations constituted from the "nondenominational," that focus on matters of practice, teaching, and interpretation. The disunity among Christians, they say, finds its roots in

---

119   Jn. 4:14

120   Lk. 22:19-20

the conflict in personal revelation and looks something like this: Suppose person A receives revelation from the divine that leads to practice P1, P2, and P3 and teaching T1, T2, and T3. Sometimes these revelations insist that a person or a group of people fraction off or splinter away from their current church in order to form a new one guided with the most recent revelation. This person might claim that God laid something upon their heart, that the Holy Spirit wants them to spread a particular message or warning to the congregation, or that heaven desires to amend current practices or teachings. Now further suppose that person B receives divine revelation too and claims its truths and insights with just as much passion and fervor as person A. As a consequence, practice P4, P5, and P6 along with teaching T4. T5, and T6 come to light. Problems arise when the fruits of revelation A given to person A conflict with the fruits of revelation B given to person B. Each claim that God spoke this or that to them and that the Spirit moved them toward this or that. How can each person be correct if their fruits contradict each other?

More concretely, there are many different sects of Christianity reflecting shared beliefs, teachings, and practices. Each sect claims to be Christian, yet the existence of such diversity from within speaks to something beyond a mere disagreement of practice and procedure. Teachings and practices in these churches contradict and conflict with one another, yet each church claims to be guided by God's hand. Each church claims to have the correct interpretation of the Bible, yet each among them disagree on the interpretation from the others! How can this be so? If there is, presumably, one God, one Authority, either He is a prankster who enjoys sowing discord and conflict in His church by telling one person one thing and another person something different, knowing beforehand that the messages are against each other, or the person receiving the divine revelation misunderstands, misinterprets, or injects his or her personal perspective into the message and claims it as divine revelation. Can you think of any other being who elevated himself above God or intertwined his essence into God's creation for his own ends and purposes? Whichever the case, the body of Christ, His church, is fractured or fraction-ed as a result with the pride of each church claiming access to the divine in a manner provided by the divine. The existence of numerous Christian sects clearly demonstrates Lucifer's influence on the body of Christ; human complacency to resolve this contradiction speaks to a general acceptance of and submission to the discord planted by Satan. At the end of the day, the faithful attend church to "feel good" about themselves as churches do not encourage Christ's followers to seek truth, ask for wisdom, and pray for a discerning heart. All that really matters is that each of them tithes money into the collection plate.

It might be best to push aside the concept of spiritual resonance for the time being and leave it to the believer to set his house in order before he attempts to teach others.[121] Many of these diverse "Christian" churches fail to resonate in truth among themselves, yet each claim exclusive resonance with the divine. Applying the fruits of this logic to the relationship between blades and whetstones would reveal whetstones who teach conflicting messages in the best case and in the worst case, their personal agenda masquerades as "universal truth." Many churches cannot and do not agree on which translation of the Bible to use; word choice, grammatical errors, semantics, and the personal agenda of the translator infiltrate the Word and is accepted as "divine approved." It is no wonder that nonbelievers maintain their distance from the Church as we would be inviting them into a divided house separated from one

---

121   Mt. 5:23-24; Mt. 7:3-5

another. Pride keeps churches apart and encourages truth seekers to make sense of it all on their own.

While spiritual resonance is unique to believers, emotional resonance and intellectual resonance are shared between believers and nonbelievers. Each brings their bodies with them to every act of consciousness, beginning and ending from the perspective of the first-person plural. Experience testifies to this. Each of them is bound to their way of seeing things, or so it seems, and each starts with the belief that others share their first-person perspective as a point of given fact, that is, every individual believes that their perspective is the only perspective and takes it as commonly accepted and understood that others in the world both share and are aware of their personal understanding, interpretation, and perspective. This natural attitude, "I see what is *really* there," that people have parallels the notion of egocentrism. "Because I believe in a thing, everyone else must believe in it too," "What appears logical to me must also appear as logical to others," "Others must share my values and everything else that I consider to be precious, important, and necessary," and "Things and ideas that make sense to me should make sense to everyone else as a point of obvious fact," they say. But these personal assertions do not align with lived experience because, as every person knows, the world overflows with diversity, contradiction, and difference. Everyone seems to be moving in different directions at different speeds, with clusters of people herding together here or there as other groups of people move in the opposite direction. The very idea of understanding, much less resonating with another person's point of view appears daunting if not impossible because of the inherent limitations and obstacles with understanding, attunement, embodiment, speech, and language. However, we must find a way through in order to experience resonance.

Informed by breadcrumbs and data points, we use our imagination as a "third-person to first-person" jump which allows us to find our way to the place of the ones whom we observe at a distance. We make a faithful effort to see the world as they see it, knowing beforehand that such a task is never perfect and that we will invariably miss some nuanced detail that may or may not change the course of interpretation. We are aware of the considerable distance between third-person and first-person and know that relational and proximal distance and interpretive accuracy are inversely proportional to each other, that is, the greater the distance, the lesser the accuracy, and the lesser the distance, the greater the accuracy. Resonance between tuning forks bears this out as well as the closer they are together, the stronger the nonstruck fork vibrates when the other receives a blow.

The risk of inaccurate understanding from a distance is worth the potential reward of growing, for if we do nothing and make no attempt to grasp the meaning secreting from the other at whatever the distance, we will never expand and fertilize our internal horizons with their wisdom; we will never expand upward and outward. Instead, without any imagined understanding, our position will harden and lock to the gaze of our natural perspective. We can either risk being alone, surrounded within our own familiar existence in safety, exerting little to no effort toward interpreting and understanding the other, or we can risk being wrong in our deductions and exposed in our incorrectness when we reach out to grasp and decipher the other. You must decide for yourself whether or not you are content and sedate with the familiar. Only you can seek to understand horizons beyond your own or seek to hide confronting and being confronted by other people. Whatever choice you make, it signifies the tapestry from which it came.

As observers, we begin by entering into a one-sided relationship with the other in the third-person from afar by studying them and by setting our gaze upon them; even though empathy's vibration remains faint and weak between us and them, it is better to start with something distant than nothing at all. We observe others and bring them into us, without their knowledge, in order to survey the landscape of their interior world as we imagine it to be within ourselves. We ask ourselves, "How must this person be standing in the world in such a way that their point of view makes sense?" We attune ourselves to the movements of the mind and passion, and to the degree that we adjust our harmonics to match theirs, we begin to understand another modality of existence. Our imagination pulls their threads, data points, and breadcrumbs into us, not as they appear as themselves from themselves, but as they appear filtered through our appraisal of them. For this reason, we strive to articulate and clarify the blemishes in our own lens before venturing out into the world ready to take others into ourselves. We then speculate how this new world inside of us makes sense to us, and by extension, to them as well. No one possesses the ability to enter into another's being to experience the world as they do with flawless accuracy; however, we are able to adjust our consciousness, interpretation, and understanding of other people so that we vibrate in resonance with them through empathy. As it is love that binds all existence together, it is only through care and empathy that we can begin to understand another person's being in the world. The closer we move toward them, and the more we open ourselves up to be affected by them, the more resonant we attune to our fellow human beings.

However, it is not our goal to "lose ourselves" in the depths of the other through profound empathetic bonding, nor is it my goal for you to lose yourself in me. I am neither your God nor am I interested in being Him. We are not seeking to surrender or substitute our individuality on the altar of someone else. Such an abdication of personhood invalidates any insights we might discover from threads, nuances, breadcrumbs, and patterns in their tapestry. It is imperative that we maintain a sense of our identity in contrast to those we bring inside to function as our perceptual lens that brings them into focus. Should we yield to their sway and allow them to take us over, our individuality would surely die similar to how sailors would jump into the sea to join the sirens. Love is not an abdication of personal responsibility, but both the purpose and apparatus that allows one to understand the other. For us, it begins with observation and imagination grounded in concrete data points and breadcrumbs.

Once we bring our appraisal of the other into us, we posit deductions about the conditions of possibility that allow one manifestation of their attunement to show itself over and beyond other potential attunements. The influence of space on our interpretations of the other alluded to earlier is now more pronounced, i.e., the transformation of third-person public space into social space, social space into personal space, and personal space into shared first-person–second-person space reflects the journey of intimacy and empathy. The distance between us and them over there reflects our third-person appraisal of their involvements, for example, our appraisal of them in the third-person becomes our investigation of them within our first-person.

To further illustrate this point, dear observer, suppose that you are at a party, hidden in the crowd as is sometimes your disposition. Now imagine seeing a person there, likewise camouflaged in a sea of faces, who spots their significant other entering the room. Each of them was unaware of the other's attendance until this moment, and now only one is aware of the other. When the hidden partner spots their significant other, he or she begins to stand to move closer to them. But before they fully rise and compose themselves, they see their partner approach a handful of people. The onlooker, not wanting to interrupt, sits back down and observes his or her significant other interacting with other people while sipping on a glass of some beverage. We observe the observer.

He or she witnesses his or her partner talking with other people and overhears the consequential laughing and sees smiling shared between them. Certain words and phrases between them cut through the noise in the room to reach your ear, and you know that if you could hear them, the other observer could hear them as well: "Hahaha, you're so funny!" and "I can't believe you just said that!" These are generic statements, to be sure, but notice their effect upon the observer.

The observer's eyes roll and you hear them sigh as they melt further into the couch. The silent partner's initial response to what they see unfolding before their eyes might be jealousy or a passive acceptance. It might be something else. "Why is my partner even talking to other people in the first place?" the observer wonders. "What could be so important that a face-to-face conversation was required here and now?" they muse. After a few moments, their significant other leaves the party in haste, leaving the silent partner to their thoughts.

The next day, the observer learns that their partner briefly attended the party to ask others about a birthday present *for them*! Their partner talked to several people at the party to gather information about the things that the observer partner might want or like—things hitherto not discussed between them. One partner wanted to surprise the other. Jealousy fades to relief. As observers observing an observer, we are not simply interested in the initial jealous response. We are interested in understanding how their emotional world is put together such that jealousy manifested itself in the first place. How does it make sense for the attunement of jealousy to manifest instead of other potential attunements, such as happiness, dispassionate concern, or blind rage? I have taught you to assume that the threads of all behavior are meaningful and reflect the tapestry from which it came. Your brief observation near the mark reveals volumes of information about them without the necessity of your interaction. Emotion carved itself upon their face, and though few to no words were spoken, you "understood" the feeling animating the behavior. Your closeness allowed you to perceive nuances imperceptible from a greater distance. Third-person observation sets the stage for second-person data collection; the more you allow others to resonate inside you, the better you will be able to grasp the facets of their existence.

To the extent that you have opened yourself to me and my words throughout our journey together, the vibration of who I am resonates within you. Our relationship together, dear observer, is found in the oscillation between second-person and first-person as a function of our proximity to one another. We began in the public space together, observing the man and the woman sitting at that table in the nightclub, and the more time we spend together and the more discussions we have together, the closer we are to the intimate destination of my design. It is my desire for you to know me. Witness for yourself the contrast between our relationship and the relationship which began our discussion.

It could very well be that in spite of our proximity to one another throughout this journey, you continue to appraise me from a cool and distant third-person perspective. You do not resonate with me at all, or if you do, you resonate faintly. You consider my words, evaluate my logic, draw meaning from me here and there, but ultimately, your heart remains closed to me. I might have written an interesting thing here and a controversial thing there, but I remain at arm's length from you.

You keep me there perhaps thinking of me locked alongside others in your friendship cage. All my words about spiritual scalpels, submission, resonance, tuning forks, whetstones, threads, tapestries, nuances, the demon legion and the relationship legion, first, second, and third person observation, interpretation, data collection, thematic unity, patterns, vulnerability, Adam and Eve, the spirit, passions, and intellect, replicants, black holes, infant abandonment, blemishes, and lenses failed to reach you or have reached you incompletely. My passion and imagination are just neurochemicals put into language. If this is the case, then this was not my first time to mistake a rock as a blade, and it will not be the last. Such is the risk that I am willing to take with those whom I perceive worthy of my time and effort.

As a sower, I must accept that not all the seeds I cast will reach fertile ground. But know that I measure "success" in the *throwing* of the seeds not in their *growth*, for that depends on the ground's ability to sustain them. In other words, you decide how the time spent with me will influence your perceptual lens. Earlier I foreshadowed that "her ability to dismiss my sincerity confines the movement of my words within her mind and heart and imposes limitations I never meant to let exist. I am as authentic or disingenuous as she desires me to be, even though I cannot be both at the same time in the same respect." I feel it my responsibility to spread seeds far and wide and I am grateful that I have been blessed with a mind and spirit capable of producing them in the first place. At the end of the day, that is all a whetstone has to show for his effort. Even the time I am given with a true blade is short-lived as any graveyard will testify.

Remember back to the beginning of this book when I predicted that, "Even if I were to convey information with perfect form supported with both scientific fact and philosophical truth, success of her understanding me is not guaranteed. Success is never guaranteed. For it is my goal for her to understand and interpret my words as I say them in just the way that I mean them." Most of the time, my prediction of not being understood comes true. The evidence rests in your absence, dear observer.

One of the most painful lessons that a whetstone learns is that not every blade is meant to be sharpened because not every blade *can* be sharpened. As a whetstone, we understand and accept that our purpose in life is to sharpen blades to prepare them for battle. We care whether their edge can pierce the enemy because we want our women in our care to survive and thrive! We see the relationship we have with blades as the recreation of the relationship between Adam and Eve; just as Adam did not want to condemn Eve to a solitary existence after sinning, we never want to turn away a blade who stands to benefit from our service. But just as Eve was free to turn her back on God's command and on Adam's loneliness, blades are free to remove themselves from the whetstone's stony table and venture out into the world with nothing more than memories of the time we spent together at most. In the least, the fallen blade might acknowledge the whetstone's investment with nothing more than "thanks." As the years roll on, however, even those memories will fade for her.

Just because I measure success in the production and casting of seeds does not mean I do not feel remorse when I see them die. Even though I do all I can in my power to ensure their survival, there are some things beyond my ability. And I never feel at ease knowing this. If I know as much as I say I do and can help as much as I believe I can, then each dead seed, to me, is proof of my impotency and failure. This happens more often than I care to admit; I remember spending time with certain blades, pouring all that I am into the effort of sharpening them only to have them misunderstand our relationship during a critical moment. When it came time for me to remove her cancer with my scalpel, she objected and claimed a violation of her autonomy. It really does not matter if the assertion was factual; the point is that the denial happened at all, and it happened within the context of the trust that led up to it. Never mind the progression of events between us over time. Never mind the long conversations, the teachings, the energy and time spent building empathy, the stories of pain and sorrow showing mutual vulnerability, and the dreams of happiness and the hope of something better than what had been in the past. Never mind the conversational intimacy where we laid naked before each other. When push came to shove, she bailed. She was, in effect, more comfortable with the idea of the cancer's removal than of the practicality of its removal. She knew that the longer it remained inside her, the more likely that it would spread to other parts of her mind, body, emotions, and spirit, until the aid needed to save her exceeded my ability to provide it. There is nothing more impotent and frustrating for me in the world than watching someone die knowing that I had the power to save them—but could not because they would not have me in the end when all indications up until that moment communicated the precise opposite.

The only way to avoid this cutting disappointment would be to withdraw from blades entirely, to recluse into myself and ponder existence from afar, lose myself in works of theology, philosophy, and psychology, and lock away and hide Adam's loneliness and its accompanying yearnings and emotions. "If Eve wants to die, let her die alone. If Eve wants to follow the serpent into pleasurable bliss, then let *it* be her whetstone. If she thinks she can find someone better who can do more for her, then let her have him, and *leave me be*," I muse to myself. But then, as I am about to close the door to my passion and retire my spirit, I hear the

Master's voice asking me to feed his sheep.[122] And I do, not because I love the blade, even though, secretly, I do, but because I serve my Master. I cast my seeds, the fruits of my mind, heart, and soul, unto the ground in servitude to Him and solemnly watch His sheep fill their bellies on the fruits of my pain only to excrete it, without a second thought, in their stride to greener pastures with tastier seeds and vegetation. Seeing my love as their excrement tires my soul.

It is like a teacher choosing to take on a student after careful consideration of the student's potential. Each enters the relationship freely and each wants to be in the presence of the other because each stand to benefit from the contributions of the other. The teacher knows that he will die one day and that if his knowledge is not passed to others, then it will be buried with him in the silent grave. Journeying toward the end in the face of inevitable death motivates him to find a willing vessel or vessels in which to pour himself. Master and apprentice, teacher and student, and mentor and trainee set the context and framework of passing the teacher's acquired wisdom and knowledge through imitation and practice under close supervision to his student. The teacher surrenders his secrets over time, the fruits of wisdom collected over a lifetime of experience wrestling with thoughts and ideas, and the student accepts them and transforms them into something she owns. His power becomes hers to control.

However, instead of seeing the journey to the end, the student loses interest and leaves the relationship. Consequently, the master doubts his ability that allowed him to perceive potential in his chosen student in the first place. Maybe he was not as smart or as perceptive as he thought he was in choosing a student who could not or would not complete the task.

---

122   Jn. 21:15-17

Maybe, he thinks, that his insights should die along with him and that he should forsake the world that turned its back on him. "If my apprentice, who spent so much time with me hearing my voice, perceiving the truth in my words, knowing my mannerisms, and resonating with my soul is able to abandon me with apparent ease, then how much easier would it be for those who do not know me to do the same? If, as a consequence of our growth together during this journey, my words have failed to reach the one closest to me, then how can I expect them to reach complete strangers through a book?"

"Sheer futility," Qoheleth says, "Sheer futility: everything is futile! What profit can we show for all our toil, toiling under the sun? A generation goes, a generation comes, yet the earth stands firm forever. The sun rises, the sun sets; then to its place it speeds and there it rises. Southward goes the wind, then turns to the north; it turns and turns again; then back to its circling goes the wind. Into the sea go all rivers, and yet the sea is never filled, and still to their goal the rivers go. All things are wearisome. No one can say that eyes have not had enough of seeing, ears their fill of hearing. What was, will be again, what has been done, will be done again, and there is nothing new under the sun! Take anything which people acclaim as being new; it existed in the centuries preceding us. No memory remains of the past, and so it will be for the centuries to come—they will not be remembered by their successors."[123]

Goodbye, my dear observer.

I will treasure the time we spent together.

---

123   Eccl. 2-11

> "
>
> *When he broke the fifth seal, I saw underneath the altar the souls of all the people who had been killed on account of the Word of God, for witnessing to it. They shouted in a loud voice, 'Holy, true Master, how much longer will you wait before you pass sentence and take vengeance for our death on the inhabitants of the earth?'*
>
> —*Revelation 6:10*

FRACTIONS OF FINITUDE

Death either comes fast or slow but it always comes. It will not be denied its prize. Human mortality sets the boundaries of existence; it is both the ultimate and the overarching limitation underneath which all other limitations appear and have context. It is the ocean that borders this island of the living on all sides. Fighting it is like wrestling with the sea and produces the same result as submitting to it. Embracing it, denying it, negotiating with it, undermining it, confronting it, or accepting it are all different windy paths, each with its own scenery, decoration, and landscape, but all eventually lead to the same destination. Like all other things both tangible and intangible, humanity inherited it from Adam and Eve and it serves as adequate proof of Lucifer's entanglement with the human soul—the reward for humanity's bond to selfishness, corruption, and rebellion. Death was not God's original intention for His creation in Eden, but it is the reality within which we all operate. Wishing and pleading to the contrary reveals yet another futile road to the same end.

How we choose to orient ourselves toward death, the ultimate future, testifies to the life we live: either we live our lives in fear, knowing that inevitable death is on its way, and therefore seek all manner of distraction to put distance between ourselves and it, or, because we know death is coming, we live out our remaining time with a sense of precious urgency to make each second count before the end. The final result is always the same regardless of how one chooses to live, however, the difference between the two approaches lies in accepting and owning one's finitude versus ignoring or denying one's eventual death. Either orientation reverse-engineers to how one conducts themselves in the world in the here and now. We are free to regret both the things we have done and the things we have not done within the horizon of ultimate acceptance or denial.

Death does not discriminate between the authentic and the inauthentic. It does not care. The one who spends their life in contemplative meditation searching for deeper meaning dies as much as the one who blunts their consciousness with drugs, who takes refuge in the past, and

who exchanges sweaty orgasmic muscle spasms for personal validation, multiplying no different than bacteria in order to fulfill evolution's
mandate. The dust of the righteous looks the same as the dust from
the corrupt and both wash away with the same effort; words etched
into their cemetery headstones contribute little more than lip service
toward their differentiation and memories of both are forever lost after
a few generations.

During life, a person brings their entire being with them to encounters with others in the world, including all of their threads and breadcrumbs, which is why I emphasized disciplined focus while striving
toward a greater clarity of perception during observations of them. People
cannot help but to reveal themselves throughout their interactions with
others and to the careful observer, relational patterns manifest after
repeated observations. But death halts the effort of all observers and
silences everything there is about a person and obliterates their future.
Death conceals all that a person could have been; at most after death,
the concentration of all that a person was in the past remains but soon
dilutes like a fragrance lost in the breeze. When someone dies, that which
defined their existence—their push toward the future, their telos, final
causality, their "for the sake of which"—also dies with them. No longer
will their voice be heard, no longer will their emotions be felt, and no
longer will they impose upon the living; their new presence is now felt
as an absence-of-presence to those who remember.

Even the remembrance by others of the one who died, filled with
loss and emotion, gradually fades as one generation replaces the next.
After about three or four generations, the dead's imprint upon the world
will be worn away like carvings in stone exposed to water and wind.
As Ozymandias rises, he also falls and his fall will last longer than his

kingdom ever did. The spaces they use to inhabit call out to them, but their master remains silent and forever distant. Pens on their desk remain arranged just as they were left, dog-eared pages in scattered books decorate a quiet table, and their unmade bed and worn pillows call to a body who will never return. Clothes hanging in the closet still smell like them, but they are nowhere to be found and their garments remain undisturbed. Pictures that went unnoticed when they were alive are brought closer to the face as the living search for some hidden meaning or intention imbued within old photographs; locking eyes with their picture in search for the fire behind their window to the soul reveals only the hollowness of pixels and the want for something more. No longer will smelling and tasting their favorite meals bring delight to their belly and their favorite drinks remained closed and unopened in the refrigerator. Silence replaces a voice that once filled a house with laughter and argument; the living would trade anything to hold them one last time. Old and worn conversations, once the cause of strife and disdain, for example, "You always say the same things," turn into concrete tokens of affection, "I wish you could tell me that same thing *just one more time*." But no. Now it is just silence. Trivialities, nuances, and character quirks once dismissed now become what made them unique and precious.

Most of those who cling to a religious or spiritual interpretation of existence find themselves motionless after death takes someone cherished. Those left behind "believe" that their beloved is "in a better place" or that he or she "is with Jesus." They might say things like, "the spiritual part of me knows that everything will be okay, but the human part of me misses them." They say these things assuming that spirit and flesh exist as some kind of mutually exclusive duality. They are not. Interesting that death easily shakes years of faith, decades of attending church, and calls into question all those private walks with God. "The spirit is willing enough, but human nature is weak."[124] Christianity teaches believers about sin and death and articulates that the life, physical death, and resurrection of Christ was part of God's plan to save humanity from spiritual death. For the faithful, physical death is a poignant reminder of their separation from the divine and serves notice that they, too, will surely die one day, regardless of their piety.[125] And even though Christianity draws a clear and distinct line between physical death and spiritual death, many Christians still feel sorrow and loss witnessing the physical death of others,[126] even though they believe in the resurrection of the dead.[127] The distance between God's will and sinful reality confronts them directly, as each is born spiritually separated from God as a consequence of inheriting Adam's and Eve's blemish, and they feel powerless to do anything about it, even though they profess love and faith in Christ. Part of each person believes that death is unnatural and foreign to the Spirit; in one final act of rebellion against death, the living weep, feel defeated and impotent, and whisper prayers on behalf of the dead.

The dead do not care, their work complete, their last breath spent or never made. Broken threads lead to the hole where they once stood, the remains of the relational nexus ripped at the fabric of their intersection. The strings of attachment that once bonded one to the other droop to the ground like a limp broken string detached from a distant kite. It is the living who must figure out how to move forward, parents without a child, wife without a husband and husband without a wife, children without their parents, friends without friends, if and when they do, for many among them find insulating comfort riding the merry-go-round of

---

124   Mt. 26:41

125   Gn. 2:17

126   Lewis, C. S. (2001). *A grief observed* (1st ed.). HarperOne.

127   Dn. 12:2; Jn. 6:40

memories, past feelings, and well-worn paths. The dead are gone but the living remain and are faced with the emptiness and silence created from the absence of the other. Guilt from opportunities not taken, regret from conversations not had, and sorrow from feelings unexpressed swirl to torment the living. Visiting their grave is all that one can do now. Apologies decorate their headstone like the various flowers left behind and silence answers the words spoken toward the ground with a gentle breeze. Why did you wait so long to speak your passion to the grass and dirt when you had the opportunity to do so eye to eye, mouth to mouth, and chest to chest when they were alive? The fear that prevented your action back then is now your companion, and "what could have been done" or "what should have been done" replaces "what was done." "All that could have been but was not" is the new thread stitching memories together.

The end makes apparent the private choices of the living heart and exposes the living's meaning-making structure. Relationships built on mutual existential fear, not faith, express themselves as an exaggerated codependent attachment between those involved. People in this kind of relationship take every opportunity to maintain and to reassure the insecure relationship either through physical touch or through virtual contact. Kissing, hugging, eating together, and sexual pleasure describe the sedative for anxiety that each injects into the other. "What are you doing right now" is the most often used phrase exchanged between these two over text messages—idle chatter. Fear of the future, fear of repeating the past, fear of growth and expanding beyond known horizons paralyze evolution of the heart and spirit. The relationship that each has with the other resembles the preceding one that each had before meeting one another. The only difference between what is happening in this one as opposed to the prior one is more sex more often; the level of accepted mediocrity, however, remains the same. The other person is an emotional blanket, a spiritual Band-Aid, and a contemplative distraction. Comforts and pleasures of the flesh describe this kind of relationship best, as it is the language that even the animals know. But whereas animals are driven by instinct outside of the realm of their control, humans involved with one another out of fear of being alone choose to limit themselves and refuse to better themselves in intangible ways.

Perhaps they simply do not know how to change or perhaps they know about the solitude, isolation, chastity, and contemplation necessary for change but consciously refuse to open themselves to these things. When one in this kind of relationship dies, the dependency that bound them together remains and the fear of solitude suppressed together through mutual effort rises to the surface to confront the one remaining. And there is no escape. The other was like a dam holding back the river of personal responsibility for their partner and now that the dam is gone, chaotic water floods in all directions, drowning the intellect and the emotions, covering action and concealing the landscape underneath. Rather than interpreting death as a wake-up call to inspire change, the remaining person panics and scatters about to find a new distraction as quickly as possible insofar as social decorum allows. In their agitated state, they consult those in the friendship cage and demonstrate their anxiety and sorrow to them as vulnerability in order to elicit sympathy from them.

Relationships established on mutual trust, vulnerability, submission, openness, and transparency, on the other hand, express themselves differently in the face of death and finitude. Because each in the relationship both acknowledges and probes limitations from the beginning, and because each are keenly aware of their mortality, the seconds shared between them mean all the more. Each lives this kind of relationship not as a succession of distractions aimed at maximum pleasure and minimum discomfort, but rather as the continual search for deeper meaning, connection, clarity, and authenticity. The other person in the relationship is a true companion who assists their partner to achieve personal understanding. Each strives to improve themselves intellectually, emotionally, and spiritually in their solitude in order to enrich both themselves and the bond they have together. Future-oriented relationships aware of death tend to be mutually beneficial in numerous ways as opposed to parasitic because the intelligence required to imagine the future translates into applying the intelligence toward other endeavors involving the other person. The whetstone wants to become a better whetstone for the sake of improving blades; the blade wants to become a better blade to showcase the whetstone's work and to fulfill his personal calling. Each wants to be the other's heavenly treasure and conducts themselves accordingly. Complementary and collaborative instead of one-sided, communicative and descriptive instead of silent and one-dimensional, and focused on the present with a future orientation instead of regurgitating the merry-go-round of the past characterize this kind of mutual and consensual involvement. While each discusses their past with the other, neither of them "live" there; analysis of the past to identify patterns enriches self-knowledge and influences adaptive behavior going forward. Each elevates the wants and needs of the other above their own wants and needs and concern themselves with helping the other reach heaven. Their relationship together is not just physical like the animals; they also express themselves being in command and ownership of their thoughts and feelings, which they share without coercion or manipulation. Their human consciousness "contaminates" their animal drives and changes the meaning behind intimate physical expression. They welcome the living embodiment of their love together manifested through their offspring, and the eventual loss of the other visits as a sadness without fear, a lamentation without heartbreak, and as a separation without loneliness. Whereas codependency expresses itself as "I fear to live without you; I do not know what I would do if you were gone," authentic relationships reflect conscious choice: "I choose to be with you; I choose to walk with you. I am glad for the time we had together and I look forward to meeting you again."

Sometimes, relationships end before they really begin as death has been known to steal babies, children, and new lovers. What was once never considered to be a viable future comes into focus and teases and prepares awareness. New parents take up the task of transforming the space inside their house and inside their heart in preparation as each begins to comport themselves toward their child's arrival. But death rips this elated anticipation away from them under the cover of night, leaving emotional destitution in its wake. The universe of possibility birthed at the introduction of a parent with their future child fades just as quickly as it began. The parent's imagined future with the child woven to it, the new imagined world with an infant inhabiting it, shatters into a thousand little pieces, and each shard incinerates into droplets of smoke. Bags of diapers remain unopened, bottles unused, and tiny socks and mittens accentuate the new space created—the baby room—with toys and gifts neatly arranged throughout for the new little visitor. Everything in this room calls out to the infant who would have and should have dwelled in it. Now all these things represent all that could have been but was not and the absence of the baby identifies their presence to the parents and to the loved ones left behind. Death robbed the potential of "what could have been" from the living and cries into the void from those who remain go unanswered; death did not just take a child but also took away all the years they would have had living and every small and great feeling threaded to it. Death usurped the parent's drive to provide and protect and stole from the lives that would have changed, for better or worse, as a consequence of the child's interaction. There are few things worse than never knowing what could have been in both matters of life and love, especially when the future of both looked so promising and bright.

The loss of a new lover is similar to the loss of a child. Both the remaining parents and the remaining lover imagined themselves inhabiting a future with the other and began creating spaces in the world and in their heart and each entertained thoughts and feelings appropriate to their desire. Each projected themselves into the future, creating the ephemeral road within the realm of the intangible using the tool of giddy expectation to make it real and tangible one day. With this goal in mind, each slowly transformed the space within the realm of the tangible, closing the distance between themselves and the potential future: the father kisses his wife's belly and pokes and prods at his child while still in the womb. He speaks comforting words and assurances to the newborn, saying that he will do his best to provide a rewarding life with lips upon her flesh.

Lovers traverse public space, social space, and personal space, to enjoy the resonance created in shared intimate space. A new Adam found his new Eve and the most recent iteration of Eve found her Adam. Each compliments the other in both matters of flesh and spirit, and upon this foundation, they begin new perceptions of the world. One day, their love will manifest itself in the flesh of their child. But death comes and takes either the man or the woman in its stride, leaving the remaining alone to hold unfulfilled desire and expectation; they become the book that no one will read, the song that no one will hear, and the film playing in an abandoned theater.

Do not allow sorrow to take you! Do not bend the knee to grief, for he is not your God! Pray for the strength to endure not for the power to avoid. Pain is part of the process and is necessary whether by scalpel or by pruning in order to bring about more fruit.[128]

Remember the following earlier words once more and consider them in combination: "Even though the dead cannot speak for themselves, our voice can unite with theirs and they can speak through our interpretations and observations *provided that we have taken the time and effort to develop our own clarity and expanded our way of thinking, feeling, perceiving, interpreting, understanding, seeing, hearing, touching, smelling, and tasting.* We can repeat and describe what they said and did in the same spirit of truth that motivated them to act in the first place." And again, "As an observer, you must develop *new eyes* to see the legions of ghosts influencing the living and *new ears* to hear their echo" Finally, "*Imagining that limits have permeability in fact makes limits permeable.* Recognizing that *our perception of limits is in itself limited and incomplete paves the way to transcend them.* Looking with purpose and desire for something different makes finding different things possible. But to the degree that one does not seek, one also does not find. And to the degree that one does not ask, one also does not receive."

The combination of these earlier insights is meant to penetrate the malaise experienced by some and to offer them a new tunnel leading out of the habitual, i.e., a new way of being always-already exists to those willing to search for it, perceive it, and act upon it. The wisdom of the dead becomes the wisdom of the living when the living takes up the same spirit of truth that animated those now dead. This spirit of truth unifies, reconfigures, and imbues the living's perceptions with a sense of urgency grounded in finitude; the fruits of the dead nourish the living. Additionally, death itself offers a profound stimulus to individuals

---

128   Jn. 15:2

sedimented in average everydayness, enabling them to "wake up" to and to call into question the patterns of their life in order to choose to change or to maintain those aspects of themselves previously taken for granted as given. Death commands them to reevaluate themselves with a certain sense of personal ownership and responsibility because each person confronts death individually. Developing new eyes to see differently and new ears to hear with clarity is paramount so that individuals take advantage of each second are not wasting precious time chasing erroneous thoughts and feelings. Death also jumpstarts the necessary desire to bring life into focus before the end as demonstrated, for example, through the story of Ebenezer Scrooge.

His acceptance and ownership of his inevitable finitude called into question his life's choices and attitudes for evaluation and both inspired and motivated him to create a new future beyond the one resulting from his negative habitual material presence to the world. The inevitability of death forced him to confront himself as he was and opened up the potential to change who he wanted to be. Confronting and accepting death after evaluating his life in terms of past, present, and future enabled him to reconstitute and reorganize his perceptual lens from cold to warm with free will. Death redeemed him, or rather, allowed him the opportunity to redeem himself. Death helped him see that acquiring status, wealth, and power means very little from the eternal perspective; performing good deeds in the spirit of charity to benefit his fellow human being, on the other hand, means so much more. "I will honour Christmas in my heart, and try to keep it all the year. I will live in the Past, the Present, and the Future. The Spirits of all Three shall strive within me."[129] For Ebenezer

---

129   Dickens, C. (1986). *A christmas carol*. Bantam Classics.

Scrooge, opening himself up to intangible matters of the spirit with free will translated into a tangible change in his presence to the world.

His profound change of heart and spirit manifested itself both as a change in his perceptual lens and as a change in his meaning-making structures. His orientation toward time, embodiment, and others shifted after he *personally* encountered death. As a result, he now considers what was once very important as less important while what was once casually ignored and dismissed as trivial and annoying as indispensable and meaningful. Before, death was something that happened to other people; his partner Jacob Marley died, yet his death did not move Scrooge to change. Only after personally confronting death did Scrooge change – and this lesson extrapolates to all human beings. We can surmise that death abstractly and death personally are two different things and produce two different results depending on its proximity to our own affairs.

Each day, thousands of people are born into the world and thousands die. We do not cry for those whom we do not know, nor do we concern ourselves beyond a passing acknowledgement that death happens in foreign lands to strangers. It is easy for us to pay it no attention, to push it out of our minds, when its focus is elsewhere and not on us. Living life would be impossible for us if we took a few silent moments to reflect upon each person's passing; to live life, death must be ignored. But to live abundantly, death must be confronted.

The limiting veil separating death from life and flesh from spirit is not as opaque as it first appears to the one more attuned the spirit than to the flesh. I am not speaking here of using tarot cards, Ouija boards, mediums, or necromancers to artificially transcend the perceptual limitations of the flesh, for these things are clearly forbidden and only serve as sly gateways for the enemy to force open the internal cracked door of sin even further for darkness and legion to invade. No, what I am saying is that new horizons open up to the one who feeds their spirit with certain food, "Human beings live not on bread alone but on every word that comes from the mouth of God,"[130] and that a new and different manner of seeing becomes possible to the one seeking it for the right reasons, for example, "May he enlighten the *eyes of your mind* so that you can see what hope his call holds for you, how rich is the glory of the heritage he offers among his holy people."[131] Just as eyes of the flesh are tuned to perceive a certain range of the electromagnetic spectrum in the realm of the tangible, eyes of the spirit are tuned to perceive matters of the spirit according to one's seeking, asking, and knocking in the realm of the intangible within God's will. We cannot, or rather, we are not allowed to perceive beyond our desire. Perceptual reality, from our point of view, reflects our intentions and to a large degree, desires and limits upon our perceptions are self-imposed and self-chosen.

A clear distinction is made between the flesh, the physical and human nature, and the spirit, the immaterial or divine nature, i.e., "What is born of human nature is human; what is born of the Spirit is spirit."[132] However, at the same time, while flesh and spirit appear at odds with each other from our fallen perspective, the whole ministry of Christ can be understood from a certain point of view as a demonstration of the proper and intended "putting together" of the Spirit in the flesh as a new "born again" creation, or, put in another manner, the proper and harmonious alignment of heaven-spirit and flesh. Jesus suggested that heaven-spirit and dust-flesh are different, yet Jesus Himself embodied the proper transformed alignment of the spirit-flesh unity. Adam and Eve

---

130   Mt. 4:4; Dt. 8:3

131   Eph. 1:18

132   Jn. 3:6

were "spirit-with-dust" and, through them, all humanity failed.[133] Jesus, however, is "spirit-with-heaven" and offers an alternative reconstitution or a new "putting back together" of the flesh and spirit to believers through Himself.[134] He reflects humanity's potential, our ultimate "will be but not yet." Death-dust mandates separation of the flesh and spirit before heaven-spirit reanimates the flesh. In other words, without death-dust, there would be no reunification of the heaven-spirit and the flesh because the "perishable" cannot put on the "imperishable."[135] Death, while sad, is necessary to produce an even greater joy—the fruits of which begin with the presence of Christ on the earth two thousand years ago.

The manifestation of God's vision through His son resonated with those select few around Him and made possible that, "The blind see again, and the lame walk, those suffering from virulent skin-diseases are cleansed, and the deaf hear, the dead are raised to life and the good news is proclaimed to the poor."[136] His chosen disciples along with those whom He touched through miracles or witness to miracles spread the good news across the face of the earth. Billions have been exposed to this new potential. The whole unfolding of human history has been one huge and necessary detour from paradise reflecting the punishment banning us from it and the forgiveness through Christ allowing our return to a new and transformed iteration of it. If nothing else, both His ministry and He Himself prove that there is a profound connection between the flesh and the spirit—that spirit has the potential to transform the very nature of the flesh—with the ultimate goal of perfect harmony and unity between

---

133 1 Cor. 15:45-46

134 1 Cor. 15:48-54

135 1 Cor. 15:1-58

136 Mt. 11:5

them from the divine perspective.[137] Those hung up on the chronological time between Christ's original ministry until now, thousands of years later, need to remember that the divine and the affairs of the divine exist outside of chronological time.[138]

Why does any of this matter? I recount these things as proof that the relationship between blades and whetstones is not simply one of two bodies interacting with one another for temporary pain or pleasure. The bond between them fills with the resonance of one human soul with another; tangible aspects of their relationship together reflect coexisting intangible or spiritual desire. Their interaction together is not simply one of convenience like the animals experience during mating season due to evolutionary and instinctual programming; there are more unseen connections ebbing and flowing between whetstone and blade that go beyond the flesh. To those who seek and ask for these things, to those who transform their eyes to see these things and their hearts and spirits to feel these things, the potential of a deep and meaningful bond comes into existence with each helping the other to move closer to the divine. To those who love without faith, these words are nothing more than additional sweet nothings and pillow talk. As it is when confronting death in a personal way, so it is when confronting love in a personal way. Both death and love either open up new possibilities to do something different and believe in something different or they will remind one to play it safe on the merry-go-round of the familiar and habitual.

If you gaze upon me resting in my coffin with eyes of the flesh, all you will see is the flesh of my hollow corpse—but I am not there. If you have trained neither your eyes to see nor your ears to hear whispering

---

137   Lk. 24:36-43

138   Ps. 90:4

matters of the spirit through desire, then all you will hear is sadness tapping at the chamber door of your heart. The divine will respect your free will. If you choose to live by the flesh, then the flesh is all that you will see because it is all you desired to see; if the divine beyond the flesh exists, do you really expect it to manifest itself to you in some act of profoundness? If it did, you surely would not recognize it, just as a two-dimensional being cannot comprehend a three-dimensional being. "Do not give dogs what is holy; and do not throw your pearls in front of pigs, or they may trample them and then turn on you and tear you to pieces."[139] Would *you* go through the effort of demonstrating advanced mathematics to a full classroom of kindergarteners just learning how to color within the lines, scribble letters of the alphabet, and craft macaroni noodle art? You would be wasting your time because children cannot perceive your efforts, regardless of your intention. Their minds are not yet ready and are not mature enough to understand such advanced things without gradual training and mastery of preceding basic concepts. And so it is with matters of love and spirit.

Becoming frustrated and disappointed with the children for being unable to understand advanced mathematics is less about them and more about you. Poor judgment allowed you to think that such an endeavor would be worthwhile in the first place. Similarly, the spirit will show itself to neither the underdeveloped nor the unwilling because they cannot handle simple things and have made no prior effort to ask, seek, or knock for understanding the intangible. From the spirit's point of view, *it* is the advanced mathematics and *you* are the kindergartener. "If you do not believe me when I speak to you about earthly things, how will you believe me when I speak to you about heavenly things?"[140] In other

---

139   Mt. 7:6

140   Jn. 3:12

words, if you cannot handle the simple, then how do you expect to handle the complex? If the spirit chooses to manifest itself to you regardless of your state of development and you are not ready for it, it will throw you from your horse, blind you, and take away your appetite.[141] Be careful what you ask for. You might just receive it.

Fellow whetstones must learn to observe correctly from a distance because there are some rocks and blades who are not yet ready to comprehend all that the whetstone has to offer. If they show no interest in approaching you, then you must be on guard even more if you advance upon them first. The distance between you and her means either that she does not resonate with you or that you do not resonate with her. If you approach first, know that you will spend a considerable amount of your energy defending your heart while attempting to explore hers. Remember, these are the rocks and most rocks have no interest in becoming blades, or at least, not your blade. I recommend that whetstones begin their observations hidden in plain sight to survey the landscape of rocks and blades prior to taking any action. If she can perceive something in you, she will come to you as a blade. You will feel the resonance. But do not waste your time waiting on a rock or blade who will never come; they are not yours to sharpen. The longer you wait for her to come to you, the longer you deny your services to those who would most benefit from them.

Remember that all perceptions occur with, through, and because of limits and that those limits are both tangible, such as the five senses, and intangible, such as the mind, spirit, and passions. If your only method of perception is through the limits of the flesh, the tangible, and the material, then all you will be able to see is the flesh, the tangible, and the material. *How you look shapes what you see.* Perceptions through, with, and because

---

141   Acts. 9:3-9

of the intangible, such as pride versus humility, greed versus liberality, wrath versus patience, envy versus kindness, lust versus chastity, gluttony versus abstinence, and sloth versus diligence reveal co-constituted objects back to consciousness colored or imbued with the mental, emotional, or spiritual status of the perceiver. For example, looking through the lens of pride reveals prideful things back to the observer and approaching the world with humility will reveal humble things. Both the apparatus *and* the method of observation define the range of what *can* be perceived, or rather, what reveals itself to the perceiver.

Many perceive life through both a tangible and an intangible keyhole, so to speak, but are unaware of the limitations and restrictions imposed by the keyhole; most people believe that their limited perspective through the keyhole reflects the totality of what rests on the other side of the door. Should the door open and they enter the room, they would find new things available to them, previously unknown and unimagined. But most are happy, sedated, and content with seeing through the keyhole; these people are a waste of time and offer further evidence to the hollowness of human beings. Perhaps some have been given the gift to work with these people; I have not. My gift is to take what a person is and make them better and sharper than before, not to convince them through clever persuasion that reality is more than what meets the eye.

If you truly desire to perceive matters beyond the flesh or other current limitations, remember the divine "ask–receive / seek–find / knock–open" relationship I described earlier within the context of how one goes about changing. I tell you that matters beyond limits exist, that there are things on the other side of the door beyond the keyhole, as our perception of limitations is in itself limited. These things dwell within permeable reach only to those who first believe with faith the size of a mustard seed that they are able to reach it. Those who do not believe will never know and are trapped within the familiar, or they do know and either accept it or experience malaise because of it. Now I pose the same question to you that the angels posed to the women at the tomb on Easter morning, "Why look among the dead for someone who is alive?"[142]

If you are interested in beginning this journey, then it must start at the end. Imagine your own death many years from now. Now imagine that as part of your funeral, individuals rise and stand before the gathering to say a few words about you. What would they say? That you were a person who kept to themselves and never risked anything? That you lived a life of comfort and ease, never challenging yourself whether emotionally, intellectually, or spiritually, and that you hid your talents in the shadows, always playing it safe, while walking the straight and narrow path of proper morality? Would they remark that you did everything other people expected of you, mistaking lazy passive acceptance of their wishes for humbleness because you never wanted to rock the boat, cause a ruckus or an uproar? Would they observe that you never expressed your dreams, your desires, or your passions so as not to impose on others? Would people presume that they were unsure of your values, goals, or opinions on topics? Do you want them to declare that you never stood out from among your peers, never made an impression on others, and never challenged those around you to become better individuals? Would you be happy knowing that you lived a life out of focus, bereft of passion and imagination, that you drifted with no plan, no agenda, and no aspiration for personal greatness?

Not only must you imagine how you want others to remember you, but you must also imagine your own death. You must do the things now,

---

142   Lk. 24:5

say the things now, while you live, in order to bring about the effect you desire upon others in the future. In the very least, you must consciously and purposely orient yourself toward the future you want to manifest and inhabit and begin to take the steps necessary to make it more likely to happen. People are neither mind-readers nor heart-readers; they only know what you show them and tell them, and even then, their apprehension will never perfectly reflect your effort. It is your responsibility, not theirs, to ensure that you effectively communicate your message to them in both deed and action. While you live, you control the choices you make to bring about your dreams and aspirations. Either you will live your life or you will be lived by it. Your death will close further opportunities to do something different; how you choose to engage your remaining time reveals how you want others to remember you and how you think of yourself.

Philosopher Friedrich Nietzsche described an interesting thought experiment along similar lines in the late 1800s. The purpose of his exercise was to have the listener or reader recount the events of his or her life and imagine repeating them over and over again, eternally, in precise microscopic detail without deviation, not necessarily for the sake of repeating the past but for the sake of creating a future worth repeating, as his demon appears during a moment in life, not at the end of life. For the one with a life well-lived without regret, repeating the succession of events in their life over and over would produce a certain sense of accomplishment and satisfaction, but for the one whose entire life was filled with half-hearted action and passive acceptance after the demon's visit, on the other hand, enduring the same succession would feel like an eternal damnation to impotency, resentment, and insecurity. He phrased his mental exercise in the following manner: "What, if some day or night a demon were to steal after you into your loneliest loneliness and say to you: 'This life as you now live it and have lived it, you will have to live once more and innumerable times more; and there will be nothing new in it, but every pain and every joy and every thought and sigh and everything unutterably small or great in your life will have to return to you, all in the same succession and sequence—even this spider and this moonlight between the trees, and even this moment and I Myself. The eternal hourglass of existence is turned upside down again and again, and you with it, speck of dust'!"[143]

One thing is for certain: mental exercises either imagining one's death or repeating one's life focus on the living's ability to change before the end. We, the living, have the power to decide how we want others to remember us at our passing and we have the power to create a new future worth repeating. Everything in your life thus far has led you to this moment to read these words; this is your opportunity to seek something different, to ask for something different, and to knock upon a different door. If not now, then when? If not you, then who? If not to expand consciousness and internal horizons of the heart, mind, and soul, then why? Will you continue to be the same person once this book has been put down? Can you return to the prison of the familiar to wrap yourself, once again, in the threads and tapestries of the past, knowing that there is more to life? Shall you return to the same keyhole as before, look through it, and continue to believe that everything you see is everything that there is to see? Shall you consume the seeds I toss to the ground to satisfy a passing hunger or will you allow them to take root, nurture them with your water and sun, allowing them to produce a new fruit tree inside your heart and mind? Will you force yourself to look at the world in the same manner going forward?

---

143   Nietzsche, F. (1974). *The gay science: With a prelude in rhymes and an appendix of songs* (1st ed.). Vintage.

At the end of the day, the choice is yours. I did what I was commanded to do. The Master whom I serve granted me certain talents and placed a degree of responsibility upon me in proportion to the gifts loaned to me in order for me to produce a profit on His investment.[144] That profit partially depends upon your receptivity to the ideas presented within the pages of this book and in the fruits of my face-to-face relationships with people outside of these pages. Receptivity depends upon the clarity of my articulation of the concepts described herein, whether religious or secular, and my treasure in heaven will be measured both in proportion to the change that these words inspire in others and in my submission to the divine through my willingness to provide these words, whether or not they take root and produce actual change. Had I not written these words, had I not allowed rocks and blades to grind upon my whetstone out of fear of being hurt once again, my Master would have held me accountable for wasting His investment. And a good servant wants to please his Master. His gifts demand responsibility. Some might say that I serve out of fear. Others might say that I serve out of love. I tell you that I serve because of both; I know my place. He is the Master and I am the student. He is the sculptor and I am the clay. I fear Him and I love Him. "The fear of Yahweh is the beginning of knowledge; fools spurn wisdom and discipline."[145]

To those of you who think that walking and talking with God is all about positive feelings, hugs and kisses, and casual discussions about the heart and spirit, you are mistaken. It is this and so much more. Perhaps the relationship begins this way for the novice, but as the relationship progresses, the lessons become more intense, He prunes more, and He expects more. But by the same token when this happens, the student is

---

144 Mt. 25:14-30

145 Prv. 1:7

capable of more and wants to provide more, can take His pruning better, and can endure His intensity better. No matter our stage of development, we are promised that we will never be given a burden that we cannot handle. "None of the trials which have come upon you is more than a human being can stand. You can trust that God will not let you be put to the test beyond your strength, but with any trial will also provide a way out by enabling you to put up with it."[146]

He disciplines and He comforts; He demands and He forgives; He leads and shows students how to follow; He is patient and He is firm and absolute. He is most definitely not a one-dimensional being and He knows what to say, how to say it, and when to say it in order to produce maximum effect. The divine's lessons never end; there is always further up and further in. Do you really think that death ends the divine teaching, that when you die, your education is complete and that you know all that there is to know? I don't think so. No one really knows precisely what happens after death or how the process of education changes, but I imagine, in the least, that "limitations" no longer include the flesh or the tangible. Understanding will no longer pass through the neuron or through the neurochemical. Knowledge through the five senses, limitations imposed by the physicality of the brain, and limitations of time, space, and embodiment will no longer apply.

Even if I knew what happens after death, it would be pointless to describe it here using the medium of human words and human ideas rooted in original sin. Neither I nor any other human being could render the description with proper justice. "What no eye has seen and no ear has heard, what the mind of man cannot visualize; all that God has prepared for those who love him, to us, though, God has given revelation

---

146   1 Cor. 10:13

through the Spirit, for the Spirit explores the depths of everything, even the depths of God."[147] I know enough to know that I do not know all about such things. What I do know is that there is more to being human than just the tangible alone, i.e., "not on bread alone,"[148] and that we require assistance in order to grasp the things outside of our limits. Human effort produces human reward; the Spirit is what binds everything together and makes possible our human effort in the first place. Reality is primarily spiritual in nature and within it, tangible reality, our experienced reality, manifests. Those with faith believe this; those without faith doubt and struggle with this.

The sun is setting.

My time is running out.

Allow me to say what I must while I still can.

Finitude begins and ends with solitude. We are born alone. We die alone. During the time in between, we either embrace solitude and loneliness or we run from them. While the divine both mandates and encourages us to participate with the larger community of believers,[149] He also expects each in the community to contemplate His word in private and to talk with Him behind closed doors, i.e., "But when you pray, go to your private room, shut yourself in, and so pray to your Father who is in that secret place, and your Father who sees all that is done in secret will reward you."[150] The divine balance between social interactions and private ones differ from person to person, according to their need and disposition, but tends to lean more toward private than social overall.

---

147   1 Cor. 2:9-10

148   Mt. 4:4

149   1 Cor. 12:12-31

150   Mt. 6:5-6

There are several reasons for this: each person is responsible for his or her own choices regardless of their social environment, each person must recognize and address blemishes in their perceptual lens and cannot assign personal responsibility to someone else, each person must seek, ask, and knock for themselves as no one can take up the effort in their place, and each person, alone, must negotiate life and death, indifference and love, and spirit and flesh and either chooses to act, fails to make a choice at all, or attempts to assign personal choice to others. Even though a person's social network contributes to their development early in life and reinforces or challenges personal conviction and belief, as the person ages, their individuality contributes back to and changes the parameters of the social. There comes a point in each person's life when they can no longer blame others for personal decisions, a time when things left unchanged are, in fact, chosen.

The relationship between blades and whetstones is a social one, to be sure, but it is also a private one. Blades consider what the whetstone does and teaches in both moments together and in private contemplation alone. Part of the sharpening process is to encourage the blade to take the lessons and conversations explored together and consider them in solitude. This is something that only blades can do as rocks tend to distract themselves from contemplating matters of the mind and spirit. Seeds planted together grow in private for the one wanting a bountiful harvest, depending on the nurture given; sharpened blades make the time to ensure that their heart's soil is fertile and well-kept, clean, and free from emotional parasites of the past.

Of all the possible disservices that rocks and blades could do to themselves, the greatest is failing to explore themselves with divine guidance in solitude. Perhaps something about female nature requires them to seek social comforts, relationships, friendships, and general social distractions. Perhaps females abhor being alone for extended periods of time—especially those endowed with beauty or cursed with it. Throughout my life, I have yet to meet a rock or a blade who has spent more than a few weeks in solitude before my involvement; most of the time, they spend their time "alone" setting up their next social engagement or relationship and never go beyond three months between physical encounters, whether "one-night stands" or formal relations with other people. They "live for the weekend" and bide their time between nights out at the club, attending parties, or visiting friends. Moments of silence and solitude at night are not spent in pensive reflection, writing their inner voice, exploring the construction of their soul or lens, working out logical solutions to difficulties, reflecting on their choices, or contemplating the mind of God. These things are to be avoided at all cost by any means necessary, whether it be through the bottom of a bottle, in the arms of a stranger or "friend," or in the smoking or snorting of drugs.

It appears that females require constant social distraction and interaction beginning in their adolescence and lasting throughout their entire life. What the boyfriends once did and got for free, the husband must now do and pay a toll. Nature and evolution reward females in their youth with fertility and beauty, and few are the ones who fail to take advantage of nature and evolution. Therefore, they spend most of their youth "having fun" and "exploring themselves," neglecting their solitude in favor of social pleasure. It seems that they meet their "future husband" around every corner and pass the crown to another as soon as the prior flame declines. They live their lives in constant motion, always seeking the next thing or person to entice them away from themselves, as they fail to identify themselves as the common denominator in all their heart break, disappointment, and sadness. As a consequence, these rocks and blades never get to know themselves, or know of themselves only through their entanglements after reflection, and never know what to do with loneliness should it ever darken their door. Whetstones are not to encourage a blade's dependency but are to foster her independence in order to prepare her for the relationship's inevitable end either through choice or death.

Social media and the personal cell phone add to their available distractions as anything is better than contemplating movements of their heart and soul under the guidance of the divine. They will wander through life not knowing themselves, afraid of being alone, and will pair-bond with all sorts of flawed and weak men when they are not bonding with strong and powerful men, whom they truly desire, whom they keep in the friendship cage. Most women will not go through the trouble of creating a replicant for their loneliness in the face of such abundant distraction. It is almost as if they require other people in order to work out their personal meaning. If their souls could manifest in the flesh and be seen with eyes of the flesh, their crippling deformities and disfigurement would chase away any onlooker. Most women know how to make love, or allow others the opportunity to make love to them, better than they know how to deal with loneliness, isolation, and solitude. These are the same women who will one day become mothers and leaders of the next generation and like the generations before them, they will not know how to embrace solitude, and their children will never learn to listen to those whispers of the divine that occur only during loneliness and isolation.

I do not claim to have the answers or know which direction to point all people in all circumstances from the beginning of time to the end. Each person is different and each whetstone is different; the words in this book are meant for a select few who have been given ears to hear what I have to say. I do not pretend that I possess the key that fits all locks. It will be obvious who resonates with the words contained on these pages and who does not. God has allowed certain people in my life and not others, with Him knowing each of our dispositions before our interaction. I do not believe in chance or accident; those whom I know are meant to be a part of my life, just as those who read these words are meant to read them. He knows my whetstone and knows that I, too, am in the process of "becoming" like the blades whom I attend.

I write from a place of love; I condemn neither rocks nor blades, for who am I to pass judgment against them? I am here to make them better and sharper in my own way—my message is not meant for all, but only for those with ears to hear it and eyes to read it. I see the weeds growing in the fields of their heart, mind, and soul and desire for each to produce a bountiful harvest. I think that in the silence and solitude of their heart, they want the same thing for themselves too. Without identifying weed from wheat, how can the bountiful harvest come about? Is there not a certain amount of labor needed to pull the weeds and tend to the wheat? Would it not be advantageous for them to learn how to identify one from the other before tending the fields in order to prevent the accidental removal of the wheat?

Keeping the past alive, resurrecting dead love in silence and solitude, maintaining a long-distance relationship in secret while being involved in a relationship already, maintaining multiple romantic attachments to multiple people without exposing personal vulnerability to any one among them, seeking distraction rather than seeking truth, yearning for physical touch rather than yearning for wisdom, relying on plausible deniability rather than relying on logic and reason, avoiding pain in order to seek pleasure, failing to reflect upon the structures of consciousness

and blemishes in the personal lens, avoiding solitude, resigning ownership over personal freedom, choice, and responsibility to others, ignoring
death and finitude, attending to the tangible above and beyond attending
to the intangible, wandering through life without a purpose, relying on
other people to provide personal meaning, becoming lost in the threads
of the familiar, settling for one uninterested in the evolution of the mind,
heart, and spirit, disregarding the fruits of observation and deduction,
running away from loneliness and emotion, pushing love, submission,
and intimate conversation away, using other people's vulnerability and
intimacy for selfish benefit, making excuses for some while making exceptions for others, denying potential, and never seeking or asking for help
to transcend personal limitation ... all these things are weeds in the field,
cancers in the soul, and the impurities blunting a blade's sharpness.

Removing these weeds one at a time is a demanding process. Using
a spiritual scalpel to eliminate this cancer from the surrounding spiritual
tissue and grinding a blade's edge along the whetstone's face takes both
time and a delicate hand. Mutual consent and mutual submission to the
greater good are necessary before moving forward and, even then, success
is never guaranteed. Every new relationship involves a degree of risk,
faith, and trust founded in each wanting something good for the other
person. Sometimes, these are enough for the relationship to produce
fruit; other times, these are insufficient, as was demonstrated through
the disappearance of my student, my companion, earlier.

"If my apprentice, who spent so much time with me hearing my
voice, perceiving the truth in my words, knowing my mannerisms, and
resonating with my soul is able to abandon me with apparent ease, then
how much easier would it be for those who do not know me to do the
same? If, as a consequence of our growth together during this journey, my

words have failed to reach the one closest to me, then how can I expect them to reach complete strangers through a book?"

THE END